THE PROFESSIONALIZATION
OF POVERTY

MODERN APPLICATIONS OF SOCIAL WORK

An Aldine de Gruyter Series of Texts and Monographs

Series Editor: *James K. Whittaker, University of Washington*

Paul Adams and Kristine E. Nelson (eds.), **Reinventing Human Services: Community- and Family-Centered Practice**

Ralph E. Anderson and Irl Carter, with Gary Lowe, **Human Behavior in the Social Environment: A Social Systems Approach** (*Fifth Edition*)

Richard P. Barth, Mark Courtney, Jill Duerr Berrick, and Vicky Albert, **From Child Abuse to Permanency Planning: Child Welfare Services Pathways and Placements**

Dana Christensen, Jeffrey Todahl, and William C. Barrett, **Solution-Based Casework: An Introduction to Clinical and Case Management Skills in Casework Practice**

Marie Connolly with Margaret McKenzie, **Effective Participatory Practice: Family Group Conferencing in Child Protection**

Kathleen Ell and Helen Northen, **Families and Health Care: Psychosocial Practice**

Marian Fatout, **Models for Change in Social Group Work**

Mark W. Fraser, Peter J. Pecora, and David A. Haapala, **Families in Crisis: The Impact of Intensive Family Preservation Services**

James Garbarino, **Children and Families in the Social Environment** (*Second Edition*)

James Garbarino, and Associates, **Special Children—Special Risks: The Maltreatment of Children with Disabilities**

James Garbarino, and Associates, **Troubled Youth, Troubled Families: Understanding Families At-Risk for Adolescent Maltreatment**

Roberta R. Greene, **Social Work with the Aged and Their Families**

Roberta R. Greene, **Human Behavior Theory: A Diversity Framework**

Roberta R. Greene, **Human Behavior Theory and Social and Social Work Practice** (*Second Edition*)

André Ivanoff, Betty J. Blythe, and Tony Tripodi, **Involuntary Clients in Social Work Practice: A Research-Based Approach**

Jill Kinney, David A. Haapala, and Charlotte Booth, **Keeping Families Together: The Homebuilders Model**

Gary R. Lowe and P. Nelson Reid, **The Professionalization of Poverty: Social Work and the Poor in the Twentieth Century**

Robert M. Moroney and Judy Krysik, **Social Policy and Social Work: Critical Essays on the Welfare State** (*Second Edition*)

Peter J. Pecora, Mark W. Fraser, Kristine Nelson, Jacqueline McCroskey, and William Meezan, **Evaluating Family-Based Services**

Peter J. Pecora, James K. Whittaker, Anthony N. Maluccio, Richard P. Barth, and Robert D. Plotnick, **The Child Welfare Challenge: Policy, Practice, and Research**

John R. Schuerman, Tina L. Rzepnicki, and Julia H. Littell, **Putting Families First: An Experiment in Family Preservation**

Madeleine R. Stoner, **The Civil Rights of Homeless People: Law, Social Policy, and Social Work Practice**

Albert E. Trieschman, James K. Whittaker, and Larry K. Brendtro, **The Other 23 Hours: Child-Care Work with Emotionally Disturbed Children in a Therapeutic Milieu**

Harry H. Vorrath and Larry K. Brendtro, **Positive Peer Culture** (*Second Edition*)

Betsy S. Vourlekis and Roberta R. Greene (eds.), **Social Work Case Management**

James K. Whittaker, and Associates, **Reaching High-Risk Families: Intensive Family Preservation in Human Services**

THE PROFESSIONALIZATION OF POVERTY
Social Work and the Poor in the Twentieth Century

Gary R. Lowe • P. Nelson Reid
Editors

ALDINE DE GRUYTER
New York

About the Editors

Gary R. Lowe is Professor and Dean, School of Social Work and Criminal Justice Studies, East Carolina University, Greenville. He is third author, with Irl Carter and the late Ralph E. Anderson, of *Human Behavior in the Social Environment* (Fifth Edition).

P. Nelson Reid is Professor and Chair, Department of Social Work, University of North Carolina, Wilmington.

Copyright © 1999 Walter de Gruyter, Inc., New York

ALDINE DE GRUYTER
A division of Walter de Gruyter, Inc.
200 Saw Mill River Road
Hawthorne, New York 10532

This publication is printed on acid free paper ∞

Library of Congress Cataloging-in-Publication Data
The professionalization of poverty : social work and the poor in the twentieth century/
Gary R. Lowe, P. Nelson Reid, editors.
        p. cm. — (Modern application of social work)
    Includes bibliographical references and index.
    ISBN 0-202-36111-x (cl. : alk. paper) — ISBN 0-202-36112-8 (pa. : alk. paper)
        1. Social workers—United States—History—20th century.   2. Social service—United States—History—20th century.   3. Poor—United States—History—20th century. I. Lowe, Gary R. II. Reid, P. Nelson. III. Series.

HV40.8.U6 P76 1999
362.5'8'09730904—dc21   99-045674

Manufactured in the United States of America

10 9 8 7 6 5 4 3 2 1

CONTENTS

Contributors

Clarke A. Chambers   Ph.D., Professor Emeritus, Department of History, University of Minnesota, and Founding Director of the Social Welfare History Archives at the University of Minnesota Libraries

Susan Kerr Chandler   MSW, Ph.D., Associate Professor, School of Social Work, University of Nevada, Reno

Leslie Leighninger   MSW, DSW, Professor and Associate Dean, Louisiana State University School of Social Work, Baton Rouge

Gary R. Lowe   MSW, Ph.D., Professor and Dean, School of Social Work and Criminal Justice Studies, East Carolina University, Greenville, North Carolina

Philip Popple   MSW, Ph.D., Professor and Director of Social Work, University of North Carolina at Charlotte

P. Nelson Reid   MSW, Ph.D., Professor and Chair of the Department of Social Work, University of North Carolina at Wilmington

Joe M. Schriver   MSW, Ph.D., LCSW, Director and Associate Professor, Social Work Program, University of Arkansas, Fayetteville

Beverly Stadum   MSW, Ph.D., Professor in the Department of Social Work, at St. Cloud State University, St. Cloud, Minnesota

Paul H. Stuart   MSW, Ph.D., Professor and Chair, Ph.D. Program, University of Alabama School of Social Work, Tuscaloosa

David Stoesz   MSW, Ph.D., Samuel S. Wurtzel Chair of Social Work, School of Social Work, Virginia Commonwealth University, Richmond

1

The Professionalization of Poverty
Common Themes and Contributions

P. NELSON REID and GARY R. LOWE

The idea of social work might seem oddly out of place in these last days of the century. Social work is an expression of optimism about the human condition and about humans in particular. It is an expression of a secularized morality that holds people responsible for the lives of others and specifically responsible for intervening in those lives in some thoughtful, "professional" way. As this is written, optimism in regard to human and social change is hardly rampant, and the twentieth century has not been altogether kind to planned social interventions, especially those most clearly related to social welfare. Today we are, as a society, skeptical of our knowledge of human behavior, we are doubtful of our ability to design effective social change, and we are suspicious of professional motivation.

However, social work has not only survived, it has thrived. It has done so by steadfastly manifesting a belief in the possibility of human and social change, by a professional commitment to practical problem solving, and by being a tireless advocate of the concept of progress as applied to human social life. Progress, as Christopher Lasch has it, involves a steady rise in the standard of living and steady incorporation of the masses into the "culture of affluence." He adds, as criticism, that progress also means an "indefinite expansion of wants" (Lasch, 1991). Social work has embraced each of these tenets, including the last, and has become a representative and advocate of the moral base of such progress.

Indeed, it has been repeatedly argued that social work should strengthen its role as the keeper and purveyor of this morality of progress, especially with regard to reducing inequality and poverty. The most recent notable case of such an argument was the publication in 1994 of Harry Specht and Mark Courtney's *Unfaithful Angels: How Social Work Has Abandoned Its Mission*. This book, widely read both in social work and beyond, argues that social workers should not be "priests in the church of individual repair" but should instead be "caretakers of the conscience of the community." Social work, according to this view, was born into a Progressive era Garden of Eden of perfect commitment to the poor and downtrodden but was corrupted by a bite of the private practice apple. The desire for professional status resulted in a turn to the middle classes as potential consumers and the offering of a cheaper psychotherapy. Thus, according to Specht and Courtney, social work "abandoned" its mission to the poor in favor of personal and professional status. In order to return to its original state of grace, social work must reject the individual client or patient focus and work through a new system of community organizations for social reform and a new era of communal social service.

As history, *Unfaithful Angels* is lacking. As we shall see in the contributions in this volume, the real history is both more complex and necessarily less clear in its moral implications. As professional myth, however, *Unfaithful Angels* is a powerful story compelling social workers to once again repent of the sin of professional avarice and medical envy and return to the one true church of solidarity with the poor and commitment to social justice. As political philosophy, and certainly as a conception of social service organization, *Unfaithful Angels* is some sort of derivative relic of the 1960s. What it calls for is virtually impossible today, one could not get there from here in this age of managed care, and it can only serve to further a sense of alienation and cultural isolation in the profession.

Thus, part of the motivation for this volume of contributions from notable scholars and educators in social work is to present a more accurate and complete picture of the character and development of the social work profession in regard to the poor than commonly presented. We do this following the one-hundredth anniversary of the establishment of the first training program in social work because we believe this is a good moment to reflect on our century-long experience. Social work is by its nature an activist field, inclined to value currency and intervention over both analysis and reflection. It is the very purpose of social work scholarship and education to correct for this understandable element of professional culture and to call the profession to moments of reflection.

As we write and compile this volume, the social work profession is in evidently sound condition. Graduates of professional programs are in much demand. The numbers of professional social workers are larger than ever, and the position of social workers in social service administration and management is better than ever. The character of social work practice, emphasizing a commitment to human problem solving and a faith in the human ability, is stronger than ever, and the research supporting it is better and more frequent. The presence of social workers across varied fields of practice encompassing health and mental health in addition to such traditional fields as child welfare suggests a strong future for the profession. Schools of social work enjoy a prominence in American higher education far beyond what has been experienced in previous decades. This is so despite the commonly held view of the past few decades as both politically conservative and excessively individualistic: hardly a cultural or political environment one would think nourishing to social work.

But, the heart and mind of social work may not be as sound as its occupational character. The practice of social work is thriving, but the idea of social work is in doubt. It is in that context that this book was conceived and it is in the service of that problem that we dedicate its content.

THEMES

As one reads the essays in this volume, the diversity of viewpoint is evident. We would obviously not all agree on the great issues of social policy presented by the presence of poverty. We would not agree on the character of the motivation of social work as a profession to either engage or disengage the poor. Nevertheless, there are certain evident themes and common threads in these essays and a core of both value and focus.

The focus of this collection is the relationship of professional social work to the poor: the poor both as an idea and as a service population. Such a relationship would seem self-evident to the public-at-large: social workers minister to the needs of the poor and ideally try to help them develop into less "dependent" individuals through the process. The reality is somewhat more complex. The majority of social workers, that is, those with professional degrees (BSW, MSW), do not work in organizations that are specifically concerned with poverty and the poor, and often those who do work with the poor have administrative or supervisory roles as opposed to direct service ones. A further reality is that social service organizations are rarely in any substantive way accountable to their low-income clientele, as a result of public or private nonprofit provision. Indeed, increasingly social services are delivered through contract with such providers or third-party reimbursement, further removing practitioners from accountability to clients. Thus, if social work has a special commitment to the poor it is not likely to be operationalized and enforced in social service organization, but rather it must be expressed and nurtured through professional culture.

It is this character of that commitment to the poor that is the focus of this volume and all the contributors seek to explore one or another aspect of that commitment. There is no doubt that early social work in the United States did have poverty as a primary focus. American social work emerged from the nineteenth-century Charity Organization movement with "scientific charity" as its operational model and social casework as its principal method of practice. After incorporating the themes, and much of the agenda, of the progressive and settlement movements, organized social work established itself as a profession specializing in the solutions of problems of dependence and deviancy. The poor, who had provided the raison d'etre for professionalization, were regarded as "reformable," the children of the poor savable, and the profession had the knowledge and skill to engage in effective reform of both poor and their environment. The development of social services related to child welfare and Mother's Aid established a pattern of public social service organization that would remain largely intact for the remainder of this century. This model would emphasize the necessity for professional control of both the definition of the problems and the delivery of the service and the profession would be effectively delegated responsibility to exercise authority and discretion in regard to the poor and dependent. Lasch says social workers of the time "saw themselves as doctors to a sick society and demanded the broadest possible delegation of authority in order to heal it" (Lasch, 1977, p. 15). Gordon adds in *Pitied But Not Entitled* that the profession accepted this mandate gladly and fought to protect it when it was under assault from New Deal reformers, who wanted to replace casework with social pensions.

One might have thought that such a history would bind social work and the poor inextricably, but there were other elements of social work development that would work against such an identity. Social work sought, with no small success, to establish itself in the image of American medicine and to found a basis of knowledge and practice independent of both the setting of that practice and the client upon whom practice was focused. Social work would specialize in promoting "improved social functioning" gained through a process of social casework organized within public and privately funded social service agencies. In addition, social work would draw heavily on the ideas and forms of practice in psychotherapy. Social reform and environmental intervention would become alternative "methods" and become part of the established community health and welfare planning process. That is, social reform was defined as creating social services that would employ social workers, and employ them not as private practitioners, a la medicine, accountable to patients, but as salaried employees accountable to supervisors, directors, and agency boards.

The casework method and theory was informed primarily by one school of dynamic psychology or another with sometimes spectacular conflicts over theory and practice in its efforts to treat the problems of the individual. The dominant professional view was one of the poor as people with problems, like everybody else, and social work knowledge and skill was neither derived from specialized study of the poor nor particularly more applicable to them.

Even with social work's expansion of its identity to emphasize social functioning in a more general sense, it would, even if ambivalent about the public provision of social services, be consistently supportive of provision of services and benefits to the poor. Despite its commitment to a method built on an individual focus and a theory of practice that emphasized human choice, the profession, especially since World War II, has supported nearly every major expansion of welfare state provision and has resisted late-century efforts at downsizing, privatizing, and reform.

Thus, over the century, social work's role has become less central to the issue of the poor. Increasingly that role is one of social service delivery, ancillary to a larger system of public social welfare provision and very much part of a mixed economy of health and mental health services. The transformation of the social services that has taken place as a result of Title XX and other forces is a dramatic one and implies a social services system for the next century that will model itself after the disaggregated, competitive, largely private and insurance-supported American health care system. Such a shift raises the issue of social work's commitment and identification with the poor that seemed so clear at the beginning of the century. Evidence of this shift and the issues it poses are contained throughout this collection.

THE CONTRIBUTIONS

Each of these original chapters deals with one or more aspects of the social work profession and its relationship to the poor. While there is no effort to provide a chronological coverage of the professions history there is a logic to the order of the contributions that will become apparent.

In the next chapter, Popple and Reid provide an overview of the history of professional social work in the United States and document the persistent search for a professional identity and model of practice. The authors point out that social work has not gracefully adapted to the major shifts in social policy toward the poor in this century and that this lack of adaptation has something to do with the apparent loss of mandate to be the "profession for the poor."

Stadum, in Chapter 3, pursues in some detail the "uneasy" relationship of social work and the principal arena for benefits and services to the poor: the public welfare sector. Stadum points out that the profession's preferences for private service provision and a practice model similar to other professions have contributed to less than an enthusiastic embrace of public welfare social work. Nevertheless, the often effective and positive nature of the relationship is noted.

In Chapter 4, Stuart discusses a criticism expressed repeatedly over the century: Social work has "abandoned" the poor in the pursuit of various practice specialties that would lead to more status and higher income. His intriguing conclusion is that a specialty-divided social work existed from the beginning and that there was no apparent "fall from grace."

Leighninger, in Chapter 5, addresses one of the most fascinating periods in both social work professional history and in American social policy, the 1960s. She explores in depth the emergence of the "service strategy" that promised to both raise standards for professional practice and expand the availability of services. Ironically the 1960s was a period in which social policy toward the poor moved away from service and toward social reform and income guarantees, thus leaving social work at the margins of subsequent developments.

The focus of Chapter 6, by Lowe and Reid, is on another pivotal period in social work history: the 1930s. The New Deal produced a rapid expansion of public welfare services at the state level and a consequent dramatic increase in demand for trained social workers. How did the profession deal with such an opportunity? The authors argue that social work's devotion to a model of professional development influenced by medicine substantially limited the ability of the profession to respond. The result was that public policy and service for the poor and social work separated with dramatic subsequent consequences.

Chandler, in Chapter 7, explores the important connections of race, social work, and poverty and concludes that the mostly white and Eastern social work leadership failed to grasp the implications of the great migration to the North as well as the total reality of the African-American experience in the United States. The result was a "weakness of analysis," an undervaluing of the "collective response" to poverty and injustice, and a certain lack of passion in pressing for reform.

In Chapter 8, Schriver provides a detailed portrait of Harry Lurie. Lurie is notable as an activist and educator over a considerable span of the century and his vision of a social work based in community work and social activism consistently stood in contrast to the "casework"-oriented social work he regarded as inherently conservative. The clarity of this vision, his ability to maintain it in the context of dramatic social and economic change, and his observations on many notable events in social work history make Lurie a fascinating study. More than that, Lurie may be thought of as representing a powerful and persistent stream of thought in social work that many in the profession adhered to, but often did not express clearly. Lurie represents the embodiment of social work's inability to come easily to terms with much twentieth-century social policy toward the poor.

Speaking of the ideological element in social work's intellectual life and specifically the sort of view represented by Harry Lurie, Stoesz in Chapter 9 deals directly with what he sees as social work's inability to come to terms with the history of the latter part of the twentieth century and the triumph of democracy and free markets. Social work, he says, has been consistently "on the wrong side of history." This persistent and romantic attachment to the left has had dire consequences and promises to continue to complicate social work's relationship with the policy and service sector and to isolate the profession even further from a central role in the problem of poverty.

We are particularly fortunate to conclude this volume with an Afterword from Professor Clarke Chambers. Professor Chambers's essay is, in his own words, "an informal reflective essay, a personal response and commentary to the scholarship represented in the separate chapters (personal communication to author). I wished NOT to be 'academic' or 'social worky,' just straightforward, logical, a bit meandering here and there, like a good conversation." His reflections provide an excellent coda to this collection by providing an important reminder of the broader perspective that must always be understood while also attempting to focus on salient distinct themes.

REFERENCES

Gordon, Linda (1994). *Pitied But Not Entitled: Single Mothers and the History of Welfare*. Cambridge, MA: Harvard University Press.

Lasch, Christopher (1977). *Haven in a Heartless World: The Family Besieged*. New York: Basic Books.

Lasch, Christopher (1991). *The True and Only Heaven: Progress and Its Critics*. New York: Norton.

Specht, H., & Courtney, M. (1994). *Unfaithful Angels: How Social Work Has Abandoned Its Mission*. New York: Free Press.

2

A Profession for the Poor?
A History of Social Work in the United States

PHILIP POPPLE and P. NELSON REID

The primary purpose of the social work profession is to enhance human well-being and help meet the basic human needs of all people, with particular attention to the needs and empowerment of people who are living in poverty.

Preamble, Code of Ethics, National Association of Social Workers

The poor have a special place in social work. This is apparent from any consideration of social work professional literature or any examination of content in social work education. It is also apparent that the general public's perception of social work is bound to the idea of poverty and service to the poor. This is so because the origins of social work are so clearly linked to the poor and the problem of poverty. It is fair to say that the emergence of the social work profession and a system for delivering social work services was the social policy response to the poor in late-nineteenth- and early-twentieth-century America. But it is also fair to observe that if all we knew about social work was what we see of social work and social workers today it would probably be health and mental health that would figure most centrally in the identity of the profession. This fall from original grace has been much discussed, most notably and recently in the widely read *Unfaithful Angels: How Social Work Has Abandoned Its Mission* (Specht and Courtney, 1994). This chapter explores how this act of faithlessness has come to pass and what the process is by which social work has become progressively loosened from its identity as a profession for the poor.

ONE HUNDRED YEARS OF PROFESSIONAL SOCIAL WORK

During the latter half of the nineteenth century due to massive popula-tion growth accompanied by rapidly increasing industrialization, urban-ization, and immigration, the United States experienced an explosive increase in social problems. The problems were massive and were increas-ing at an alarming rate. For example, at a time when the population of New York City was well under one million, police estimated that there were more than ten thousand children living on the streets; other estimates ran as high as thirty thousand (Fry, 1974). In addition, vast slum districts appeared as housing was developed for the millions of newly arrived immigrants. Indoor plumbing, hot water, and good ventilation were rare, and under such conditions disease spread easily. Infant mortality was the highest in U.S. history. Earnings were low and working conditions often brutal. Millions of children worked alongside adults in factories, in mines, in the field, and on the dock. Efforts by organized labor to deal with such problems were met with violence and injunction, leading to a sense of class conflict on a grand scale. The United States was in a state of social dis-order and its most basic institutions seemed threatened economically and politically.

In response, a middle-class "revolution" of sorts occurred, in which nei-ther the industrial capitalist nor the labor leader would be dominant, but rather the professional, educated, urban class would assert control over both the definition of social and governmental problems and the proposed solutions to them. This would be called the Progressive movement, encompassing a cultural and educational agenda as well as a political one, and its impact on the United States would be enormous. Three social movements active in this period would form the basis for the development of a social work profession that would assume responsibility for the poor and dependent: the Charity Organization Society Movement (COS) begin-ning in 1877 in Buffalo; the settlement house movement beginning ten years later in New York City; and the child welfare reform movement, rep-resented most notably by the Children's Aid Society and the Society for the Prevention of Cruelty to Children, both also based in New York City, but with more progressive versions quickly emerging in Boston.

The settlement house movement and the child welfare movement would make important contributions to the development of the social work profession, but it is in the Charity Organization Society Movement that the true origin of social work is to be found. The settlements and the child wel-fare agencies had rather limited and concrete aims. The settlements wanted to be "neighbors" to the poor and to help communities solve self-identified problems such as day care, literacy, and citizenship. The child welfare agen-cies were concerned with "rescuing" children from inadequate homes or from the streets and finding wholesome living situations for them. Once this was accomplished, the agencies considered their job done. The settlements rejected the idea of expertise, and the children's programs, at least initially, rejected the idea that they were social welfare agencies, preferring to identify with law enforcement. The COS movement had more ambitious goals. The COS people not only sought to assist the poor, they wanted to understand and cure poverty and family disorganization. The name the movement quickly adopted for itself, scientific charity, summed up the attitude. The Charity Organizations wanted to apply the wonders of science to do for social welfare what this approach had done for medicine and engineering. They wanted to study the problem of dependency, gather data, test theories, systematize administration, and develop techniques that would lead to a cure.

The COS movement was a response to the rapid growth of relief-giving agencies, the lack of coordination among them, and the absence of any guiding principles for decision-making about people in need. The relief situation was perceived to be excessive and chaotic. The COS leaders sought to replace the existing system of charity with one rational system that stressed investigation, coordination, and personal service. Each case was to be considered individually, thoroughly investigated, and assigned to a "friendly visitor," who would get to know the family and would help it solve the problems that had led to its dependency. The COS friendly visitors are the true foreparents of today's social workers.

THE COS DEVELOPS THE ENDURING MODEL OF SOCIAL WORK: 1890–1915

Like the majority of nineteenth-century social welfare agencies, the Charity Organization Societies were originally staffed primarily by volunteers. Each COS had a small paid staff, called agents, who were responsible for taking applications for relief and for collecting and verifying information about each case. Indicative of the importance that the COS attached to standardization and record keeping, the clerical staff generally outnumbered the administration and agents combined. The information that was collected by agents and recorded and organized by the clerical staff was then turned over to a volunteer board, who would make decisions regarding the applicants' eligibility for assistance, what kind and how much, and would assign the case to a volunteer friendly visitor. The friendly visitor was not concerned in any way with the dispensing of relief but rather was concerned with providing treatment, or personal service as it was then called. Because the COS agencies originally viewed the causes of poverty as almost entirely moral (vice, indolence, intemperance, etc.), the major treatment technique consisted of providing a positive moral example of clean and prosperous living. As stated in annual reports of an early COS, "Marvelous indeed it is to find in how many cases some cause of poverty and want exists which you can remove! . . . You go in the full strength and joy and fire of life; full of cheer and courage; with a far wider knowledge of affairs; and it would be indeed a wonder if you could not often see why the needy family does not succeed, and how to help them up." The techniques utilized by the friendly visitors consisted of personal attributes such as "all possible sympathy, tact, patience, cheer, and wise advice" (Lubove, 1965). Thus the COS people believed that it was not enough to relieve want and suffering with the provision of material assistance, but that it was actually possible to remediate the causes of dependency through the medium of personal service.

Within a very short time it became obvious that there were serious problems with relying on volunteers for the provision of social services. One problem was simply that of numbers; there were never enough volunteers to meet the needs of all the COS clients. An 1893 survey found that the shortage of visitors was so great that fewer than one case out of seven was ever seen by a volunteer (Lewis, 1971). The more important problem, however, was that of expertise. The friendly visitors initially went into the homes of the poor thinking that a cheerful nature, a willing spirit, and a good example would be sufficient to solve their problems. What they often found, however, was not families in need of moral example and guidance, but of "exemplary piety" and diligence overwhelmed by circumstances beyond their control (Lewis, 1971). As a result of these problems, by the late nineteenth century the charity organizations began to replace volunteer friendly visitors with paid staff and the agencies and staff began to search for knowledge and techniques that would enable them to be effective in their fight against poverty and dependence.

By the 1890s there developed among COS personnel a strong desire to establish their work as a profession. There were several reasons for this. The first is that professionalization was a major social trend during this era. Medicine and engineering had demonstrated the wonders that could occur when science was applied to practical problems through the vehicle of a profession and, as a result, people began to view the development of new professions as the answer to many modern problems. It appeared reasonable to think that the myriad and diverse social problems plaguing the new urban society should be the proper target for solution by a new profession. A second reason for the strong desire for professional status among charity workers was related to the fact that their jobs had begun as volunteer positions and agency boards had a tendency to view them as still being volunteer positions to which a small stipend was attached. As most charity workers were people who needed to earn a living they were very interested in establishing the idea that their work was deserving of a living wage. Gaining recognition as professionals would accomplish this. A third factor behind the initial impulse for professionalization among charity workers was related to the status of women in American society in the late nineteenth century. A new class of women was emerging who were well educated and wanted careers outside the home. The traditional professions were largely closed to them and they were seeking alternative avenues for success and achievement. Developing charity work into a full-fledged profession where they would not be blocked due to their sex was a good strategy. Finally, paid charity workers, like the volunteers before them, were discovering the immense complexity of the task they were facing. They began to firmly believe that helping people deal with social problems such as poverty and family breakdown was a task every bit as complicated as those dealt with by physicians, lawyers, and engineers. Agency administrators were finding that poorly educated people, or people with less than top-notch abilities, were failures as charity workers just as one might assume that they would be failures at traditional professions. The result of all of these factors was that by the late 1890s a powerful movement was gaining momentum to develop training and research centers and to demand that people doing charity work be trained and recognized as professionals.

The first step in the effort to establish charity work for the poor as a profession was the establishment of training schools. In 1893 Anna Dawes published a paper titled "The Need for Training Schools for a New Profession." Dawes argued that a good deal of knowledge and expertise was being accumulated by people with experience in charity work and that some formal mechanism should be established to allow experienced workers to pass this along to new workers so they would not have to repeat the mistakes of their older colleagues. In 1897 the COS leader Mary Richmond published a paper titled "The Need of a Training School in Applied Philanthropy." In it she said of people entering charity work, "Surely, they have a right to demand from the profession of applied philanthropy (we really have not even a name for it) that which they have a right to demand from any other profession—further opportunities for education and development and, incidentally, the opportunity to earn a living" (Richmond, 1897).

Following the publication of the papers by Dawes and Richmond, along with many similar statements, and the beginning of in-service training by organizations such as Boston's Associated Charities, formal professional education was begun in 1898 under the sponsorship of the New York Charity Organization Society. This effort, called the Summer School of Philanthropy, was six weeks long and consisted of lectures, visits to public and private charitable agencies and supervised, fieldwork. In 1903 the program of the school was expanded to include a six-month winter course; in 1904 it was extended to one full year and the name was changed to the New York School of Philanthropy. Other cities quickly followed New York's lead and established professional schools for the training of charity workers: the Chicago Institute of Social Science in 1903, in Boston the School for Social Workers in 1904 (the first to use the profession's new name), the Missouri School of Social Economy in 1907, and the Philadelphia Training School for Social Work in 1908.

By the early years of the new century charity work had been firmly established as a full-time paid career, and training schools had been established out of the recognition that the functions performed by charity workers were complex and demanded formal training backed up by research. The new profession was rapidly beginning to be identified as social work, and the more professionally oriented segment of the profession, the COS workers, were beginning to think of their specialty as social casework to differentiate it from the work being done by the settlements, which was perceived as less professional in orientation. At this point, casework began to expand outside the traditional setting of the charity agency. As Lubove (1965) has observed, during these early years of the century social workers' "employment in several institutions whose effectiveness had been limited by a failure to consider the social environment of clients or patients was a decisive episode in the evolution of social work as a profession." In 1905 medical social work was established at Massachusetts General Hospital under the sponsorship of Dr. Richard C. Cabot for the purpose of studying "the conditions under which patients live and to assist those patients in carrying out the treatment recommended by the medical staff" (Trattner, 1989). Beginning in 1906 public schools began to utilize social workers to establish linkages between the schools and the students' social environments. In 1913 boards of education began to confer official recognition upon school social workers, and in 1921 the prestigious Commonwealth Fund included school social work in a five-year Program for the Prevention of Delinquency (Lubove, 1965). In 1906 Dr. James Putnam, chief of Massachusetts General Hospital's neurological service, after observing the work of the Social Service Department in the hospital, created a specialized division in the department to deal with mental patients. He hired three people to visit patients' homes and the results provided for Putnam a "fresh endorsement . . . of the value of skilled friendly visiting and the careful study of home conditions as a supplement to the physician's work among dispensary patients and as a means of making his directions to them effective" (Lubove, 1965). Thus by 1910, social work had developed identifiable specialties and had already begun to define itself as having a rather more generic mission than simply one of providing systematic relief to the poor.

THE FLEXNER REPORT AND THE TURN FROM BOTH
SOCIOLOGY AND THE POOR

By 1915 social workers were beginning to feel confident that they were members of a new and potentially powerful profession. However, a debate had been active for a number of years as to what the major focus of the profession should be. One faction, those with intellectual roots in the settlement house movement, believed that the new profession should focus on the social causes of dependency. Leaders of this group, such as Samuel McCune Lindsey at the New York School of Social Work, Edith Abbott at the Chicago School of Civics and Philanthropy, and George Mangold at the Missouri School of Social Economy, argued for a profession based on social and economic theory and with a social reform orientation. Mangold (1917) wrote:

> The leaders of social work . . . can subordinate technique to an understanding of the social problems that are involved. . . . Fundamental principles, both in economics and in sociology are necessary for the development of their plans of community welfare. . . . Courses in problems of poverty and in the method and technique of charity organizations are fundamental to our work. But the study of economics of labor is quite as important, and lies at the basis of our living and social condition. . . . The gain is but slight if our philanthropy means nothing more than relieving distress here and helping a family there; the permanent gain comes only as we are able to work out policies that mean the permanent improvement of social conditions. (p. 89)

On the other hand there were a number of social work leaders, generally with their roots in the COS and related treatment-oriented agencies, who believed that the new profession should concentrate on the development of practical knowledge related to addressing problems in individual role performance. The COS leader Frank Bruno argued that social work should be concerned with "processes . . . with all technical methods from the activities of boards of directors to the means used by a probation officer to rectify the conduct of a delinquent child" (Bruno, 1928, p. 4).

In 1915 the program planning committee of the National Conference of Charity and Correction invited Abraham Flexner, an educator who had gained international renown for a study of medical education that had resulted in a massive improvement in the quality of medical care and consequently in the status of physicians, to analyze the progress of social work toward professional status. Flexner presented his paper titled, "Is Social Work a Profession?" at the group's 1915 meeting. His answer to the question posed in the title of his paper was an unequivocal "no."

Flexner concluded that social work strongly exhibited some of the traits normally associated with professions—it was intellectual, derived its knowledge from science and learning, possessed a professional self-consciousness, and was altruistic. However, in several important areas Flexner found social work lacking, mainly those of possessing an educationally communicable technique and practitioners assuming a large degree of individual responsibility. Regarding social work's lack of an educationally communicable technique, Flexner felt the source of the deficiency was the broadness of its boundaries. He believed that professions had to have definite and specific ends. However, "the high degree of specialized competency required for action and conditioned on limitation of area cannot possibly go with the width and scope characteristic of social work" (p. 585). Flexner believed that this lack of specificity seriously affected the possibility of professional training: "The occupations of social workers are so numerous and diverse that no compact, purposefully organized educational discipline is possible" (Flexner, 1915, p. 588).

In the area of individual responsibility Flexner felt that social workers were mediators rather than responsible parties.

> The social worker takes hold of a case, that of a disintegrating family, a wrecked individual, or an unsocialized industry. Having localized his problem, having decided on its particular nature, is he not usually driven to invoke the specialized agency, professional or other, best equipped to handle it? To the extent that the social worker mediates the intervention of the particular agent or agency best fitted to deal with the specific emergency that he has encountered, is the social worker himself a professional or is he the intelligence that brings this or that profession or other activity into action?

The Flexner "bomb," as it has been dubbed, had a massive and immediate impact on social work. Social workers consciously set out to remedy the deficiencies identified by Flexner, mainly the development of an educationally communicable technique. Social casework with individuals, families, and small groups had always been the major interest of the social workers who were most interested in professionalization and so it is no surprise that this was the area emphasized in response to Flexner. The committee charged with responding to Flexner's paper reported, "[T]his committee . . . respectfully suggests that the chief problem facing social work is the development of training methods which will give it [a] technical basis" (Lee, 1915, p. 598). The committee felt that the social work profession had the beginning of an educationally communicable technique in the area of social casework and the profession should narrow its focus to emphasize this.

In the years following Flexner's paper, social workers earnestly sought to correct the deficiencies he had identified. The number of professional schools rapidly expanded, a professional accreditation body was formed, pressure was brought to standardize curricula, training was recommended for all workers, and a series of conferences was held to develop and promote the idea that casework was a singular, generic skill, regardless of setting. Mary Richmond published *Social Diagnosis* in 1917 and published *What Is Social Casework* in 1922, which together were seen as providing the educationally communicable technical basis for the profession that Flexner considered to be so vital.

The result of all these activities was that by 1929 social workers, following Flexner's criteria, had narrowed the definition of social work to psychiatrically oriented casework building on the European developments in dynamic psychology. In the process of doing this they had all but eliminated public welfare, social and labor reform, as well as "less professional" techniques such as liaison and resource mobilization. They had also eliminated techniques practiced by settlement workers such as group and community work. Roy Lubove observes that "like Flexner, social workers failed to realize that the opening of lines of communication between individuals, classes, and institutions, and community resource mobilization could be defended as legitimate 'professional' responsibilities" (Lubove, 1965, p. 107). What social work had accomplished, though, was substantial: an identity widely recognized as professional, a method of practice applicable to a wide range of human problems, and an extensive educational and professional structure supportive of its further development.

THE DEPRESSION AND NEW DEAL: A RETURN TO THE POOR?

In 1929 an economic depression began that was to prove to be the longest and deepest in American history. By the end of that year the value of securities had shrunk $40 billion. Hundreds of thousands of families lost their homes, millions of unemployed walked the street, and tax collections fell to such a low that schoolteachers could not be paid in many areas. The United States had faced depressions before, in 1837, 1873, and 1893, but these had each lasted only a few years. The Great Depression of 1929 was to last a full decade (Nevins & Commager, 1966).

The depression had a rapid and profound effect on social work. Prior to the depression the vast majority of social welfare services, including financial assistance, were administered by private agencies. Most social workers felt that private welfare was vastly superior to public welfare because public agencies were thought to be corrupt and inefficient and, therefore, were not settings conducive to professional practice. Following the election of Franklin Roosevelt in 1933, this situation changed rapidly. The Social Security Act, passed in 1934, moved financial assistance as well as much of public health and child welfare to the public sector. In response to

the development of public programs and the expansion of the social welfare system, the number of social workers increased from forty thousand
to eighty thousand, the majority of whom were employed by public
agencies.

In addition to the great increase in the number of social work positions,
and the change from private to public auspices, the nature of the social
work jobs and the characteristics of the people filling them changed during
the depression. Prior to the depression social work was well on the way to
becoming an all graduate-trained profession. Schools of social work had
been steadily moving from granting certificates or baccalaureate degrees to
granting only the MSW degree. The nature of the social worker's task was
coming to be defined as mapping and modifying the complex intrapsychic
landscape of clients, i.e., providing skilled casework services based on a
thorough understanding of psychotherapy. The clientele of social agencies
was including an increasing number of the nonpoor. With the coming of the
depression this situation rapidly changed. The massive growth of jobs was
almost exclusively in the public sector and involved helping basically well-
adjusted people deal with problems brought about by unemployment, and
most of the new jobs were defined by state civil service boards as requiring
only a BA degree, often even less.

As Lowe and Reid describe elsewhere in this volume, in the face of this
massive growth of social work jobs in the public sector the social work profession held fast to its goal of becoming an all graduate-trained profession
providing skilled casework services based on psychotherapeutic theory
and technique. Rather than a new social work emerging from the depression, one encompassing both public and private agencies and both professionally trained and lower level workers, what emerged was two separate,
but overlapping professions. Graduate social workers, while accepting
public welfare as a legitimate field of practice, were unwilling to accept
people without graduate training as professional social workers. The
mostly BA-level social workers employed in the new public welfare
programs were not allowed into professional associations, and schools
offering undergraduate-level social work training were not granted accreditation, or even recognition, by the association of professional schools. As a
result, public welfare workers generally joined unions, if they joined anything, and colleges with undergraduate social work programs joined
together and formed their own association for the purpose of support and
accreditation, the National Association of Schools of Social Administration
(Leighninger, 1987). Many professionally trained social workers felt that
because welfare was now the responsibility of public agencies, the social
work profession no longer needed to be concerned with it and could get
back to what they perceived as the core of social work—the psychological
adjustment of the individual to his or her social reality.

PROSPERITY, MENTAL HEALTH AND
SOCIAL FUNCTIONING, 1940–1960

The huge demand for goods and services caused by the Second World War brought an end to the depression, which the Roosevelt administration's New Deal programs had succeeded in ameliorating but not ending. The period of the war and postwar era was one of prosperity and optimism, unfortunately accompanied by attitudes of complacency and governmental conservatism. The prevailing attitude in the country was that the problem of poverty was rapidly disappearing in, to use the economist John Kenneth Galbraith's (1958) term, the "affluent society." To the extent that poverty still existed, most people, including many social workers, felt that it was being dealt with by the public welfare system and was therefore little cause for concern.

Social workers felt once again free to concentrate on the individual causes of distress and on developing knowledge and techniques to deal with these. A number of developments also tended to push social work even further in this direction. The testing of millions of military recruits during the war had revealed a prevalence of mental health problems greater than anyone could have imagined. The result of these findings was a push for mental health services, which resulted in the National Mental Health Act in 1946 and in the establishment of the National Institute of Mental Health in 1949. This act stressed community-based treatment and prevention and provided new opportunities for social workers interested in psychopathology.

The psychotherapeutic orientation that had begun in the 1920s, and that was de-emphasized in the 1930s, found wide acceptance in the 1940s and 1950s. This approach made sense not only to social workers but also to people who supported social agencies. The general feeling of the era could be summed up as a belief that the social system works, that therefore problems are due to some defect of the individual, and that therefore the appropriate approach is to find and cure the defect. During the 1950s, 85 percent of students in schools of social work chose casework as their major. This interest in individual counseling was reinforced by the fact that more and more persons above the poverty line were turning to social workers for help. A 1960 study of family service agencies revealed that 9 percent of clients were upper class and 48 percent were middle class (Leiby, 1978).

Accompanying the return to interest in the individual causes of social problems was a successful effort by graduate schools and graduate-trained social workers to reassert their dominance over the profession. In the early 1940s the social work unions died out, leaving the sub-graduate-trained social workers without an association to represent their interests. In 1955 following a lengthy negotiation, seven associations of social workers in specialty areas merged to form the National Association of Social Workers (NASW). Social workers without the MSW, generally employed in the public sector, were not welcome. In a similar fashion the National Association of Schools of Social Administration, the accrediting body for undergraduate programs, and the American Association of Schools of Social Work, the graduate accrediting body, merged to form the temporary National Council on Social Work Education. The council sponsored a major study of social work education, the 1951 Hollis-Taylor report, which recommended that social work education be confined to the graduate level. As a result the temporary association was replaced in 1952 by the Council on Social Work Education (CSWE), which accredited only graduate programs. The effect of the demise of the unions and NASSA and the rise of NASW and CSWE was to define sub-graduate-trained social workers once again out of the profession. This was in spite of the fact that over three-quarters of people occupying jobs defined by the Bureau of Labor Statistics as social work positions did not have graduate training in social work.

THE 1960S: POVERTY "DISCOVERED" AGAIN

Throughout the fifties the country had been lulled into a false sense of well-being by books such as Galbraith's *The Affluent Society,* which argued that poverty was a small and declining problem. People in America who were poor were thought to be so either because they lived in areas isolated from the general economic prosperity of the country (insular poverty), or because of individual problems that prevented them from functioning as viable wage earners (case poverty). As the new decade began, the country was shocked by a series of books, articles, and reports demonstrating that poverty still existed in America on a massive scale. Notable among these were Michael Harrington's *The Other America* (1962), Dwight McDonald's "Our Invisible Poor" (1963), and the report of the Ad Hoc Committee on Public Welfare appointed by the new Kennedy administration. The result of these events taken together, plus a general feeling in the nation that we had been stagnating and change was needed, was a tremendous interest in the problem of poverty and public welfare moving to the forefront of policy concerns for the first time since the depression.

The new interest in poverty was demonstrated during the 1960s by three major programs launched by three different administrations. Each of these programs envisioned a different role for the social work profession but each had the effect of reaffirming the profession's commitment to public welfare and to widening the scope of social work practice to well beyond the narrow intrapsychic focus of the fifties.

The Kennedy administration successfully proposed the 1962 amendments to the Social Security Act, popularly known as the Social Service

Amendments. These amendments were chiefly concerned with providing social services to welfare recipients to help them solve whatever problems were preventing them from being self-sufficient and specifically identified the social work profession as the appropriate provider of these services. The act provided for the federal government to fund 75 percent of the cost to states of providing social services to welfare-eligible clients, allocated money for states to send welfare department personnel to school to obtain MSW degrees, and provided money for schools of social work to develop and staff curricula in public welfare.

While successful in increasing the interest and involvement of the social work profession in public welfare, the Social Service Amendments represented the traditional casework approach of providing individual services to help people lift themselves out of poverty. Little attention was seemingly directed toward altering the social conditions that caused the poverty, although the Kennedy administration would proceed with other avenues, for example, the Manpower Development and Training Act of 1962, that would arguably benefit the poor. It is also interesting and significant that although federal training funds were specifically intended to professionalize public welfare via assisting public assistance staff to obtain the MSW degree, state welfare departments rarely used the funds for this purpose. The majority of employees sent to graduate school were child protective service staff, who worked in an area that welfare departments themselves were trying to define as not being an antipoverty program.

The Johnson administration, assuming power after Kennedy's assassination, would build on the work of a Kennedy task force to propose and pass the 1964 Economic Opportunity Act. The EOA, one of the most interesting and ambitious examples of American social policy, emphasized social reform to expand social opportunities for the poor. Billed as a major piece of the "war on poverty," it abandoned the welfare state model of social benefits in favor of community organization for social action and stressed the involvement of the poor themselves in the process of decision-making about programs affecting their lives. "Maximum feasible participation," as the policy was called, contributed to the polarization of the poor, which was apparent in regard to race in any case, and led to political confrontations in many cities. The War on Poverty programs were concerned with empowering, rather than repairing the poor. These programs initially ignored professionals, indeed were generally hostile to them, under the theory that the poor would develop "indigenous" leadership and would be the experts in determining what they needed. Over time, social workers became more apparent in these programs as the early days of high reform gave way to the inevitable program administration and service delivery realities, as "cause" became "function" in the classic formulation of Porter R. Lee (1929). The intellectual effect of the War on Poverty, and the cultural and political context of the 1960s, was great and

the social work profession would move quickly away from a nearly exclusive focus on the individual to a much wider focus on the social and economic causes of problems. Motivated by this policy thrust, most schools of
social work added community organization, social policy, and planning to
their curricular offerings and a more general emphasis on social criticism
and social reform.

The Social Service Amendments were not successful, however, in stem-
ming the rapid increases in the public welfare roles, nor was the Economic
Opportunity Act for that matter. Faced with this apparent lack of success,
and with a swing of the nation's mood toward political conservatism, social
reform was no longer in vogue. By 1967 the Social Security Act was once
again amended, this time emphasizing "hard" services such as the Work
Incentive Program (WIN), day care for recipients who were employed or in
job training, and instituting a formula whereby a welfare recipient's grant
was reduced by only a percentage of earned income when that person
became employed.

By the end of the 1960s, social work found itself in a position of considerable distance from both policy formation and service provision for the
poor. This was a result of the combined effect of the choice not to respond
to the increased demand for trained public social service workers in the
1930s and the apparent failure of expanded social work services as provided in the Service Amendments in the early 1960s. This was followed by
an era of distrust of authority and professionals and a more general political radicalization in the mid- and late 1960s. The totality of these things
was devastating. The profession was in no position to respond to the new
direction of social policy for the poor represented by WIN and the Nixon
administration's Family Assistance Plan. Rather than embracing the work
incentive model as consistent with expanding opportunity for the poor
and increasing support, the profession, through the NASW, fought the
policy direction and embraced the politically discredited "guaranteed
income" approach. This marginalized the profession in regard to policy
for the poor and further alienated the profession from the central aspects
of the American policy and service system for the poor. Thus the profession that began as one specifically mandated to deal with the problem of
poverty had by 1975 come largely unmoored from its origins in regard to
the poor and had definitively rejected the public mandate to serve the poor
in terms of accepted public policy.

SOCIAL WORK EXPANDS ITS DOMAIN

While social work has not been a central actor in the formation and
implementation of public policy regarding the poor in the last third of this

century, it has nevertheless made efforts to become more inclusive of those workers who provide the services to the poor in a wide range of public agencies. Since 1970, social work has taken major steps to include more people within the definition of the profession. In 1970 NASW changed its membership requirements to allow people with baccalaureate degrees from approved programs to become full members. This change required that some mechanism be developed to approve undergraduate programs and this was accomplished in 1974 when the CSWE began to accredit Bachelor of Social Work (BSW) programs.

As a result of including baccalaureate social workers in the definition of the profession and the corresponding increase in the number of people receiving this credential, nearly half of the five hundred thousand jobs that the Bureau of Labor Statistics identifies as social work jobs are now filled by people with professional credentials, a proportion much higher than at any previous time in social work's professional history. BSWs have not necessarily taken prominent places in the profession but with nearly four hundred undergraduate programs accredited, as opposed to about 128 graduate MSW programs, the balance is certainly shifting.

Ironically, as the NASW and CSWE have expanded the definition of professional preparation and have become more inclusive, the character of social service delivery and organization has dramatically changed, meaning that the stereotypical ideal of the BSW—a career public social service worker in child welfare or public assistance—is a thing of the past. This is so for a number of reasons. One is the expansion of the mental health and health service sector, which has become the major area of social work employment. Social workers may work with the poor in such settings but such health and mental health programs are in no way specifically antipoverty in purpose. That clients or patients are poor is a contextual aspect that surely shapes practice, but the basic knowledge and skill involved in such services is not specific to the poor.

Another element in the undermining of social work's identity with services for the poor is the increasing use of contracting with smaller nonprofit or for-profit agencies and firms to deliver social services to specified populations "on time, on budget, and in protocol." Traditionally social work had been practiced in either governmental or private not-for-profit agencies. A few social workers, especially after World War II and most especially in large metropolitan areas, had established a private practice, usually in some aspect of mental health. But in recent years this private practice has both grown and changed so that practice in private fee-for-service settings or for-profit firms has become commonplace. Private fee-for-service refers to a practice organization typical for professionals such as physicians and lawyers, where a social worker "hangs out a shingle" and provides services, generally counseling or therapy, on an hourly rate basis. The growth of licensing laws and the corresponding expansion of many insurance and government benefit programs to include social workers as eligible for reimbursement have greatly accelerated the expansion of social workers in private practice. Private for-profit businesses that employ (or are owned by) social workers and that have expanded in recent years include drug and alcohol treatment programs, nursing homes, eating disorder clinics, adult day-care centers, and companion services.

The development of private practice and for-profit social work has met with a mixed reception in the profession. Many welcome these developments and believe that the establishment of a private base for social work practice permits more autonomous and hence more professional services, and also creates additional career opportunities and makes the profession more attractive to potential social workers. On the other hand, a number of people in the profession view the development and expansion of private for-profit social work as a cause for concern. Reamer, for one, observes, "In increasing numbers, social work is attracting practitioners with limited commitment to the profession's traditional concern with social justice and public welfare" (1992, p. 12).

One might argue that the private market allocation of social services, undoubtedly undergirded by insurances public and private, constitutes a more efficient and effective way of delivering services than the old public service monopoly model. Indeed, every nation seems interested in copying many aspects of America's move to privatization in public and social services. But Reamer's observation is undoubtedly valid. The larger ideals of social justice and public welfare will become subordinate in the new social work to ideals that have to do with the effective delivery of specific services in an accountable way: more evaluative research, more budgetary accountability, more specialization, and less ideology and broad welfare-statist rhetoric.

Social work's decreasing emphasis on services to the poor is, to a certain extent, a reflection of twenty-first-century market realities. Social work is not the only profession with a claim to competence in the area of human services, and higher levels of competition from other professions will only increase in significance. The area of marriage and family counseling is a good case in point. Historically family services have been a cornerstone of the social work profession. When public welfare departments were established in every state during the Great Depression, the Charity Organization Societies shifted their focus from providing material relief to providing skilled family counseling. These agencies were, for many years, the exclusive province of graduate-trained social workers. In recent years, this situation has begun to change. Departments of Family and Child Development, and departments of Counseling Psychology, at a number of universities have begun to offer specialization, often at the doctoral level, in marriage and family counseling. The primary accreditation body that has emerged for family counselors is the American Association of Marriage and Family Therapists (AAMFT), which includes a number of people with social work training, but in no way identifies with the social work profession. Perhaps the most ominous development occurred in 1990 when *Social Casework,* one of the oldest and most prestigious professional social work journals, changed its name to *Families in Society.* The editorial introducing the new journal never mentions the social work profession, but instead talks about "creating a new journal that reflects developments in the *human services professions*" (Burant, 1990; italics added). In some states, Michigan for example, social workers are not even eligible for licensure as marriage and family counselors without additional training outside schools of social work. If current trends continue, and it appears that they will, marriage and family therapy will become less, rather than more the exclusive domain of social work. Family counseling services are to an ever increasing extent provided through the auspices of managed-care companies, companies that are interested in cost-effective and efficient services, that have little interest in dealing with a "profession for the poor."

On the other hand, social work has renewed its association with another traditional area of service and this one with a strong public service tradition: child welfare services. Through the middle of the century, child welfare was considered to be a social work specialization and social work was clearly the dominant profession. Over the years since, however, due to a number of developments, notably the drive to declassify public positions to make staffing of public agencies easier and cheaper, the traditional alliance between social work and public child welfare was weakened. During the 1980s and early 1990s, however, a series of legal judgments involving the rights of children in foster care established that children in protective service have a right to professional services. Such cases have typically required states to greatly increase the number of social workers in the child welfare system, consequently hiring more professionally trained (BSW and MSW level) workers and supervisors. As a result, state social service departments and schools of social work have formed what has come to be called the New Partnerships initiative. Funded through the U.S. Children's Bureau, this initiative has stimulated a renewed alliance between public child welfare services and social work education and professional organizations. But child welfare is not an antipoverty program in the usual sense nor is child welfare associated, as it was in the past, with any sort of benefit structure for poor children. It is perhaps significant to note that the renewed interest of the social work profession in public child welfare has occurred simultaneously with the narrowing of child welfare to a nearly exclusive focus on abuse and neglect, and a corresponding de-emphasis on child welfare as an antipoverty area. Kamerman and Kahn have surveyed state child welfare agencies and found that the activities of these agencies now focus primarily on investigating allegations of abuse and neglect, and providing treatment to substantiated cases. Families with less severe problems, including income insufficiency, are not accepted for services (1990, pp. 9–13). Thus, social work's reinvolvement in child welfare is occurring accompanied by a redefinition of the practice specialty as one providing treatment services to a pathological population, regardless of income level.

Thus social work has come to the end of the twentieth century with little more than a sense of history, a continuing rhetoric of poverty, and a thread of child welfare services connecting it to the poor. As we have shown, social work rejected its early-century mandate to serve the poor both by failing to educate those who did and include them in the professional family, and later by rejecting the broad outlines of public policy toward the poor that slowly but inevitably moved toward a work-based, not family- or child-based, benefit system. In a sense this may be regarded as a product of forces within the profession that we might regard as representing both the "left" and the "right." From the left came the ideology of the welfare state with its abhorrence of means-tested programs and its admiration of large-scale, social insurance—like benefit programs. The "guaranteed income" idea fit this ideology well and led to a view of mainline public policy toward the poor as one of stinginess and judgmentalism. From the cultural right came the recognition of the importance of professionalism and the attendant status and authority. Social work wished to define itself, and to be viewed, as a profession and it understood that it could not do so with a narrow definition of itself specific only to the one social "disease" of poverty. Rather, it would present itself as a profession concerned not with the poor but with the problems of "social functioning" and as such its knowledge and skill could be applied to a broad range of persons and problems.

In the larger sense, however, it is not possible to place the blame for this failure of nourishing the professional mandate entirely on social work. Professions do have specializations, they do have a focus on clients and patients, they do think in terms of cases and "treatment," they do have educated members who aspire to some measure of social status and sense of accomplishment, and they do have to respond to markets. But more than that, the idea of poverty and the poor has changed over the twentieth century. As Stoesz discusses elsewhere in this volume, and many have noted, the ideological and political structure supporting social work and a "profession for the poor" has largely collapsed. As Kreuger (1997, p. 22) puts it, social work has suffered the "disintegration of its grand narratives," a fate he puts to the death of Marxism as a model for understanding social inequality and for informing social policy.

Thus, social work has not and, indeed, could not have survived as the "profession for the poor." Its future must clearly rest on some other raison d'etre. This is, after all, what the profession of social work has clearly wanted: a professional identity that does not rest on a specific problem, or a category of people, but a "method" or process of professional service applicable to the broad range of human experience. The current character and great variety of the practice roles available to social work, not to mention the high demand for professional social workers, attests to its success as well as its likely future strength. Nevertheless the problem of its raison d'etre and the unity of the profession persists.

REFERENCES

Bruno, F. (1928). The project of training for social work. *Adult Education Bulletin, 3, 4.*

Burant, Ralph J. (1990). Welcome to *Families in Society. Families in Society: The Journal of Contemporary Human Services, 71, 3.*

Dawes, A. (1893). The need of training schools for a new profession. *Lend-A-Hand, 11, 90–97.*

Flexner, A. (1915). Is social work a profession? *Proceedings of the National Conference of Charities and Corrections* (pp. 576–590). Baltimore, MD: Russell Sage Foundation.

Fry, A. (1974). The children's migration. *American Heritage, 26, 4–10, 79–81.*

Galbraith, J. (1958). *The Affluent Society.* Boston: Houghton- Mifflin.

Harrington, M. (1962). *The Other America: Poverty in the United States.* New York: PenguinBooks.

Hollis, E., & Taylor, A. (1951). *Social Work Education in the U.S.* New York: Columbia University Press.

Kamerman, S. B., & Kahn, A. (1990). If CPS is driving child welfare—where do we go from here? *Public Welfare, 48, 9–13.*

Kreuger, L. W. (1997). The end of social work. *Journal of Social Work Education, 33*(1), 19–27.

Lee, P. R. (1915). Committee Report: The professional basis of social work. *Proceedings of the National Conference of Charities and Corrections* (pp. 597–600). Baltimore, MD: Russell Sage Foundation.

Lee, P. R. (1929). *Social Work as Cause and Function and Other Papers. Proceedings, National Conference of Social Work* (pp. 2–20). New York: New York School of Social Work.

Leiby, J. (1978). *A History of Social Work and Social Welfare in the United States.* New York: Columbia University Press.

Leighninger, L. (1987). *Social Work: Search for Identity.* New York: Greenwood.

Lewis, V. (1971). Charity organization society. In R. Morris (Ed. in Chief), *Encyclopedia of Social Work* (16th ed., pp. 94–99). New York: National Association of Social Workers.

Lubove, R. (1965). *The Professional Altruist: The Emergence of Social Work as a Career*. Cambridge, MA: Harvard University Press.

Mangold, G. (1917). *The Challenge of St. Louis*. New York: Missionary Education Movement of the United States and Canada.

McDonald, D. (1963). Our invisible poor. *New Yorker Magazine*, January 19, pp. 82–132.

Nevins, A., & Commager, H. (1966). *A Short History of the United States*. New York: Knopf.

Reamer, F. G. (1992). Social work and the public good: Calling or career? In P. N. Reid and P. R. Popple (Eds.), *The Moral Purposes of Social Work: The Character and Intentions of a Profession* (pp. 11–33). Chicago: Nelson-Hall.

Richmond, M. (1897). The need of a training school in applied philanthropy. *Proceedings, National Conference of Charities and Correction* (pp. 181–188). Boston: George H. Ellis.

Richmond, M. (1917). *Social Diagnosis*. New York: Russell Sage Foundation.

Richmond, M. (1922). *What Is Social Casework?* New York: Russell Sage Foundation.

Specht, H., & Courtney, M. (1994). *Unfaithful Angels: How Social Work Has Abandoned Its Mission*. New York: Free Press.

Trattner, W. (1989). *From Poor Law to Welfare State: A History of Social Welfare in America* (4th ed.). New York: Free Press.

3

The Uneasy Marriage of Professional Social Work and Public Relief, 1870–1940

BEVERLY STADUM

INTRODUCTION

This chapter tells the story of the first decades of "modern" welfare policy and practice, in the late nineteenth and first half of the twentieth century in the United States, and the simultaneous and related story of the evolution of professional social work. The brittle relationship between social work and the public social services for the poor was developed in these decades and the nature and substance of that tenuous and uneasy marriage says much about the character of the profession.

THE PRIVATE VS. PUBLIC TENSION

From early in the current century, two social welfare phenomena have existed, are well-known, and are much interpreted: (1) the expansion of responsibilities within the state and federal government, and (2) the evolution of professional social work as a predominantly private social welfare activity against this backdrop of ever-increasing public relief activity. These two phenomena intersect at the point of dispersing public relief. Social workers' attitudes have changed over time, from an initial stance in the nineteenth century of labeling public welfare a scourge to be rid of, to their organizing during the 1930s to promote its expansion.

During the six decades discussed here, as now, reforms for dealing with the poor promised more than they could or would deliver, with financial relief, employment, and casework vying as solutions. This debate was heard in cities where charity organization societies (COS) were first instituted, in state campaigns to pass mother's pension legislation, and in congressional committees designing a federal response to the Great Depression. While the arena for their actions expanded, social workers consistently made the argument that "who" was a professional and "what" was social work were revealed in the "how" of handling financial assistance. To be effective, the dispensing of relief required standards, because discrete dispersal of effective relief was based on knowledge about the recipient and trained intervention in his or her circumstances. That is, the value of relief was associated with its administration. Though limited in affecting the *formation* of public relief policy, professional social workers' influence appeared in the mundane *implementation of public as private relief.* Social workers' daily activity and career moves carried them back and forth between the presumably separate spheres of government and voluntary sectors (Katz, 1986).

The history of social workers' implementation of relief reveals apparent differences and divisions between urban and rural settings and from one state to the next, reflecting the significance of states' rights in shaping not only social welfare benefits but the venue for professional development. In addition, it is apparent that private charity agents or social workers did not speak with one voice. Social work, like other professions, included people with varying levels of education, inclination, and influence. All of these factors have contributed to the split that still exists between professional organizations whose members are employed in the voluntary service sector and those with membership in public welfare settings.

THE SHORTCOMINGS OF PUBLIC RELIEF AND PRIVATE CHARITY IN NINETEENTH-CENTURY COMMUNITIES

The institution of public relief, its assertion as a legal and humanitarian responsibility of government, its funding through taxation, its implementation at the hands of local officials, and its less than adequate provision for a selective group of recipients amid fears of dependency had a secure foothold in the evolving United States long before social workers began to define themselves as professionals. Puritans brought welfare principles drawn from the English Poor Laws. As early as 1642, officials in Plymouth, Massachusetts, listened to discussions in town meetings about the virtues and needs of those whose "incompetence" might qualify them for the receipt of "outdoor relief." Two hundred years later, in towns, townships, parishes, and counties all over the country, local election or appointment established someone akin to an overseer who decided who might receive the meager provisions defined as "relief."

Reading nineteenth-century county relief records, Michael Katz (1986) determined that relief went principally to the most vulnerable: widows, children, old people, and the sick. However, resistance to this public responsibility is indicated by the fact that legislatures in fewer than half of the states originally *mandated* relief. Other states authorized relief only at public discretion and only as a last resort after the exhaustion of reliance on self, on family, and on private charity. Nineteenth-century voters were essentially males who owned property, and were frequently uneasy with obligations that drew on local property taxes (Brock, 1984). In sharp contrast, both politicians and the general public endorsed state and federal funds for veterans' pensions, which purported to honor the past and to bear no resemblance to needs-based assistance for the poor (Skocpol, 1992).

As an expanded population and volatile nineteenth-century economy applied upward pressure on relief expenditures, opposition became a popular element in political campaigns. The governing social philosophy endorsing public obligation to help the *truly* unfortunate was overcome by the belief that relief victimized *both* the public and the recipients. While some critics realized that relief rarely did more than prevent starvation, more lamented how it destroyed self-reliance, threatening community morals and leaving business, the engine of progress, short of workers as they preferred the dole to honest wages (Axinn & Levin, 1975; Lubove, 1968).

By midcentury, complaints about the cost of relief and the character of its recipients were superseded by confidence that the solution to a needy population was construction of county poorhouses ("indoor relief" as opposed to the material assistance of "outdoor relief") so as simultaneously to shelter and reform the impoverished. Even after construction of such institutions, the delivery of outdoor relief persisted, as did the poor. By the end of the century, civic leaders preached a scientific, systematic approach to reducing poverty, implemented by *private* agencies, superior to the proliferating random activities of existing charities.

Nineteenth-century middle-class women, freed from certain household labors by prosperity and emboldened by the religious impulse of the age, acted on the social definition of female virtue by establishing private missions charities and benevolent societies whose efforts went beyond the informal assistance that had previously sustained communities for centuries. Anne Firor Scott (1990) characterizes the archetypal woman from a benevolent charity as someone who visited another woman "bearing food and clothing in one hand and a Bible in the other" (p. 37).

By the late century, thousands of benevolent organizations and philanthropic individuals were making independent decisions about in-kind relief, usually for women and children, often tied to some provision of education, employment, religious training, or health care. Such charity crossed paths with public relief when an official asked a private benevolent organization to help a worthy applicant whose particular need precluded public aid; in turn, the society could lobby for assistance for a household.

The largest private program of the time, though not a charity per se, was New York City's Association for Improving the Condition of the Poor (AICP), which organized volunteers to visit poor homes, carrying the message district by district that temperance, hygiene, and education were the avenues for rising out of indigency. The agency handbook explained, "The most effectual encouragement . . . is not alms . . . but that *sympathy* and *counsel* which re-kindles hope" (Trattner, 1994, p. 71; emphasis added).

Civic leaders of the time did not find the unregulated economy responsible for poverty, but chose instead to criticize indiscriminate charity and the inferiority of the lower class as "proven" by pseudoscientific studies. Many believed the solution to poverty lay in reform efforts combining the personal rehabilitative approach of the AICP and citywide organization like the COS for rationalizing private efforts.

RELIEF: "ONLY" A TOOL IN FAMILY CASEWORK

The concept of the COS spread nationwide, its adherents motivated by varying combinations of distrust of the administration and impact of existing public relief, disillusionment with poorhouses, compassion for the poor, and fear that the presence of the poor undermined democracy. A standard COS formula promised to control urban poverty via a centralized registry of supplicants and an objective investigation to determine and match need with the assets of cooperating charities. The final remedy would come through a caring relationship with volunteer visitors. First in Buffalo in 1877 and then elsewhere, a local COS, typically named United or Associated Charities, became a community's most prominent private social welfare agency and eventually the incubator for professional social case work (Watson, [1922] 1971).

Enthusiastic discussion about the COS model spread through the National Conference of Charities and Correction (NCCC; begun in 1873 and renamed in 1917 as the National Conference of Social Work, NCSW), a gathering of persons from the state boards overseeing relief and institutions. At this annual venue for discussing social ills and remedies, agency workers oriented toward treating families one by one and social reformers urging structural change in economics and politics met as distinct but overlapping and often conflicting groups (Walker, 1933).

COS advocates butted against public relief with confidence in the superior methods of private charity. Josephine Shaw Lowell, a steadfast nineteenth-century social reformer who used private family funds to help establish the New York City COS and supported its development under

Edward Devine's administrative hand, steadfastly opposed direct relief as a remedy for poverty and dependence and used public officials' own testimony to argue against it in her important book, *Private Charity and Public Relief* ([1884] 1971). Consistent with views like those promulgated by leaders such as Lowell, New York's superintendent of the poor was quoted as saying that relief educated "bright, intelligent children" to become "paupers or criminals"; and the Wisconsin State Board of Charities asserted that "a large amount for poor relief does not indicate a large amount of suffering . . . but a large amount of laxity or corruption on the part of officers" (Lowell, [1884] 1971, pp. 56, 57).

By the century's end, negative publicity and COS pressure led certain large city governments, including New York and Baltimore, to end public-supported municipal relief, leaving the needs of the poor in the purview of the COS (Warner, 1894). While many southern cities, for example, New Orleans and Atlanta, had always been reluctant to fund public relief, COS advocates accused officials in Pittsburgh and Los Angeles of being too "lavish" with the public treasury and thus contributing to poverty (Devine, 1905). At the 1900 National Conference the director of the Buffalo COS presented survey results of relief practices nationwide, revealing that in cities where a poor tax was levied, private charity donations, the source of COS funding, fell when compared with contributions from people living in cities free from public taxation (Warner, 1894). Aside from any private vs. public philosophical issues, variables such as the economic ones reported by the Buffalo COS director indicated that for the COS movement to succeed in its mission, it needed to be rid of public relief.

Against the backdrop of the public/private debate, the nature of private charity was evolving and its problem-solving approaches toward low-wage households, ill health, and dangerous housing were seen to require, at times, material relief and advocacy in addition to personal cheer or moral admonition. Therefore, nascent social workers affiliated with the COS became service providers rather than simply organizers of other agencies' assets (Wenocur & Reisch, 1989). These forces served to promote an awareness that charity work required more than an altruistic motivation and a kind heart.

CASE WORK PRACTICE WITHIN PUBLIC RELIEF

As COS agents/family caseworkers investigated poor families, they learned how men's death, injury, illness, incarceration, and particularly desertion left women to manage on their own. Miserly wages and the demands of child care allowed scant opportunity to work outside the home and still be caring mothers. Child welfare advocates expressed alarm when destitute parents felt no option but to place their youngsters in institutions. At the White House Conference on Youth in 1909, this dilemma was related to the importance of home life for the nation's well-being (Bremner, 1971).

Over the next few years, middle-class women's organizations engineered a nationwide campaign for pensions to enable mothers to be home with children (Leff, 1973). For some in social work, this seemingly humane and even patriotic initiative raised old doubts about public relief. Proponents of the efforts to keep mothers and their children together took care to differentiate between mothers who served their nation by child rearing and indigent males or paupers on the public dole.

Passage of the first state pension laws led to lively debate at the 1912 National Conference. Some acknowledged that private resources fell short in helping families and thus *public* relief for widows was needed, while others proposed that any new public relief funds be administered by the trained staff of private agencies (Committee on Families and Neighborhoods, 1912). Jewish charities actively endorsed pensions but others in private agencies shied away from expansion of *public* support which seemed to be relief, except in name, and which established a *right* to assistance independent of skilled assessment of its circumstances (Ladd-Taylor, 1994; & Trattner, 1994). Well-known COS leaders, primarily in eastern cities where public relief had been eliminated and who were most closely affiliated with the Sage Foundation, actively opposed the pensions. However, agencies and practicing caseworkers were not entirely of the same mind; some registered concern that opposition to legislation led to "bad press" for social work.

Luminaries such as Mary Richmond stated the existing ambivalence in the following way: "We are all agreed, I think, that families are being broken up which should be kept together," but she was also convinced that personal service and individual care were essential to lift families permanently out of impoverishment, and that the developing social work profession offered that service (Richmond, 1913; Bell, 1965).

For many critics, the *public* aspect of pension administration threatened the program. From the nineteenth century, people handling public relief had been characterized as ignorant and unreliable at best and politically corrupt at worst. Among the civic goals of Progressive reformers was the effort to neutralize urban machine politics characterized by cronies, deals, and purchased votes. One aspect of machine politics was politicians' providing episodic back-door, in-kind assistance. The association of this version of relief with corrupt politicians was viewed as an obstruction to the judicious service of social workers (Skocpol, 1992). Few people wanted mothers' pensions to become enmeshed in the political spoils system that accompanied Civil War pensions. Yet the campaign's revelation about the difficult straits families were in implied that private COS/ family agencies had fallen short in their relief and reform mission and a new remedy was required.

Mothers' pensions legislation passed easily, and by 1921 forty states in the urban North and West were routing new public dollars to families via miserly benefits. Coverage, however, was spotty owing to state statutes giving counties a choice in participation, and details undermined rights. The social biases of legislators and female pension advocates combined with the unpopularity of taxation and led to limited eligibility based on the *cause* of a mother's lone status (Abramovitz, 1996). That is, women had to qualify on character rather than just need in order to assure payment from the public investment. Michigan sought, for example, "proper guardians" and Montana required a "fit person morally, mentally, physically" (Skocpol, 1992). The universal "suitable home" requirement meant that determining eligibility and monitoring family behavior required case investigation and intervention akin to processes practiced by personnel in private agencies (Leff, 1973; Pumphrey & Pumphrey 1983; Abramovitz, 1996). Critics within social work who had feared that public pensions would provide money without attention to the development of family life were vindicated.

Nationally, thousands of additional public dollars began to flow to families, more in the urban than rural areas, and more to widows than other dependent mothers. However, according to Ladd-Taylor (1994), "most poor women were ineligible for aid or lived in counties that provided no pensions" (p. 19). Benefits were routinely set below estimates of need and many communities spread a little money to all eligible families rather than support any decently.

While the mother's pension recipients could theoretically be assisted out of need by effective social casework, no such assumption existed about the elderly. Pensions for mothers promised to separate them from the scandal of bad working conditions and the stigma of relief. In contrast, older workers' lack of competitive status in the labor market encouraged the consideration of old age pensions as an acknowledgment of contributions already made.

Mother's aid was subject to very uneven quality in administration, but pensions for the elderly and blind frequently were handled by officials responsible for the maligned outdoor relief. While the three categorical programs differed from state to state, by the end of the 1920s state and local taxes funded more relief than did voluntary contributions to local community chests distributed by social workers in private agencies (Geddes, 1937). Yet in the minds of many private agency professionals, the scurrilous nineteenth-century overseer and the ward boss helping impressionable voters remained strong images that distinguished public assistance from their own activity. However, in the largest urban areas and progressive states, public employees were identifying themselves as social workers.

PROFESSIONALIZATION IN PUBLIC RELIEF WORK
OF THE 1920s

In the 1920s the title "social worker" accompanied employment in a social welfare setting rather than formal training or task (Lubove, 1965). The general public, as well as many social workers, were uncertain about the parameters defining social work, but efforts were under way to claim specific authority for social work comparable to that of other professions.

By 1921 social work education, reflecting a strong casework orientation emanating from the 1917 and subsequent Milford Conferences, existed in approximately twenty schools including the influential New York School of Social Work, where Richmond had first discussed scientific charity organizing. Also, in 1921, the American Association of Social Workers (AASW) was established with membership based primarily on experience, but its agenda stressed the need for a definition of appropriate practice and training.

A different curriculum with less casework emphasis emerged most notably in Chicago, where Sophonisba Breckinridge, holding a law degree and a doctorate in political science, and Edith Abbott, with graduate training in economics, expanded the Chicago School of Civics and Philanthropy into graduate education at the University of Chicago. These two women pioneered in research on public relief administration and encouraged students into this arena for professional practice (Costin, 1983; Muncy, 1991). Graduates from Chicago and the other schools, along with people who lacked formal education but had experience, moved into supervisory positions in state and urban public welfare programs as well as to local agencies and national organizations.

During the 1920s, Edith Abbott helped design changes in Chicago's public welfare office. There, and in Kansas City, Cleveland, St. Louis, Dallas, and other cities, boards of public welfare subsumed the old departments of poor relief along with such services as indigent dispensaries and free legal aid. In 1923, Mary Richmond wrote, "The day may come when public family welfare departments can assure a greater continuity of policy (and that policy [being] progressive) than the private agency can. When that day arrives, I shall favor making a large part of our present family social work activities public" (Brown, 1940, p. 53).

Parallel to these urban changes, progressive state governments, Massachusetts and Pennsylvania among them, were centralizing social welfare functions and demanding more accountability from county officers. Roy

Lubove (1968) called this process a "revolt" against the long-standing negative reputation of public social welfare. A newly "scientific" viewpoint linked relief to other social factors and advocated trained employees. "Public welfare officers" and "welfare commissioners" were replacing "overseers"; "poor relief" or "outdoor relief" became "general relief" (Lubove, 1968).

In tracing the emergence of public welfare policy, however, Blanche Coll (1995) found that relief in small towns and county seats persisted as a "sideline" for county commissioners, justices of the peace, and township trustees. Many states had ended their harshest poor law provisions, but rural assistance was minimal and record keeping, seen by trained social workers as an indication of professionalism, was "crude" with "haphazard" administration allowing the possibility of petty graft. Only a third of the states had welfare activities throughout all counties; in many areas poor law legislation allowed only the distribution of either cash or in-kind service. While the Red Cross had sent trained social workers and volunteers into many small communities with services for soldiers' families during World War I, social work often was suspect (Lubove 1965).

SEEKING FEDERAL RELIEF

By the end of 1930, members of the AASW executive committee had published a statement on "The Responsibility and Contribution of Social Workers in Unemployment Crises," asserting that only the government, rather than private agencies, could handle the economic emergency presented by the depression. In the field, however, many social workers hesitated from claiming a political position, believing it inconsistent with professional objectivity and unwarranted, if employment improved.

In 1931, thirty-five hundred social workers filled conference sessions with talk of the previous winter's unemployment and future uncertainty. Reporting on the conference in a long article entitled "The Challenge of Hard Times," appearing in the *Survey* (1931), Springer captured the concern and questions of conferees about the mission of private agencies and public relief. The article revealed a range of fears held by conferees including the fear of federal appropriations for direct relief alongside the fear that federal funds would not be forthcoming. Further, there was the fear that developing social work philosophy would be drowned in the swelling tide of public relief; the fear that public activity would not go far enough, that standards of work would go overboard, that professional status would be lost, and finally, that the newly fledged profession would be unequal to its first big test.

In another conference presentation titled "Refocusing Family Casework," Gordon Hamilton (1931), once Mary Richmond's protege and, at the time, on the faculty of the New York School of Social Work and active in the new American Public Welfare Association (APWA), proposed that the depression was encouraging professional clarity. Family agencies had shouldered much responsibility for relief, but most rejected being identified as relief agencies and staff members used casework methods that drew "more from the psychologies rather than from economics or sociology. . . . Now we see that relief is not something which can be replaced by case work, nor is it something that must always be accompanied by case work" (Hamilton, 1931, pp. 176–187). While trained workers in *both* private and public agencies might offer relief *and* family work, the crisis presented by the depression began to reveal social work's limited capacity for resolving poverty.

Social workers' experiences throughout the next year (1932, the worst year of the depression) pushed many in the social work establishment to believe *federal* assistance was "necessary" and "inevitable"; and at the next conference, little time was given to discussion about casework practice. The 1932 November election was yet to occur and federal action for relief was months away.

SOCIAL WORKERS' EFFORTS TO INFLUENCE
FEDERAL RELIEF POLICY

On the eve of the depression, the federal government was spending millions on veterans and occasionally helped communities stung by natural disaster. For example, in 1928 aid to veterans and their dependents consumed 96 percent of the three-quarters of a billion dollars making up federal relief, and a third of the remainder was allocated for "Indian wards" on tribal reservations. Issues of unemployment were not addressed as an immediate concern and with the onset of the depression, the emphasis on private-sector solutions continued to drive relief efforts. President Herbert Hoover invited prominent social workers to sit on committees considering the economic crisis. Hoover was most amenable to *non* governmental suggestion reflecting the very clear orientation to voluntary solutions rather than public.

By 1931, most social workers had shaken their prejudices about the inferiority of public relief, but were still not ready to call collectively for a program of *federal* relief. In New York City, however, the social work community was poised to act. Staff at national reform organizations located there had long advocated a broader federal role in social welfare. These individuals, along with Paul Kellogg from the *Survey* and social workers from the city's hard-pressed service agencies put aside their skepticism of Tammany Hall politicians and cooperated to encourage more *municipal* relief, then demanded and got *state* action by New York's governor Franklin Roosevelt, and urged *federal* unemployment relief.

This activity and subsequent discussions led to the creation of a Social Work Conference on Federal Action on Unemployment (SWFAU). The SWFAU was formed to gather information, develop proposals, and secure "a hearing" for a social work point of view in Washington. The larger organizations underwrote the cost of operation, but membership was personal, and no one assumed the conference spoke for all social workers. An AASW subcommittee was also created on Methods of Administration of Federal Aid for Unemployment Relief with Joanna Colcord as chairperson. Writing in *The Compass* (1930) she emphasized that any forthcoming government relief action "should avail itself of the cumulative experience of the profession of social work" (p. 206).

Members of the Committee on Federal Action felt more opportunity to influence the administration after Franklin Roosevelt won the presidency in 1932 and they lost little time in approaching the new administration with proposals. For many of them, activity in New York's partisan politics and social service network had included relationships with Eleanor Roosevelt, Frances Perkins, the new secretary of labor, and Harry Hopkins, Roosevelt's chief relief administrator. Social workers offered advice to Hopkins in drafting the Federal Emergency Relief Act (FERA) of May 1933, which authorized five hundred million dollars; half went to grants to enable each state to develop and fund local emergency direct relief and work relief programs in addition to any existing general relief or categorical pensions. With FERA under way, private agencies also saw costs go down. In certain urban areas where one-third of the country's population lived, the private share of relief dropped from 24 percent of the total in 1929 to 1.3 percent in 1933.

At the next National Conference in 1933, social workers heard Hopkins (1933) call FERA "experimental," saying Congress intended relief primarily for the *unemployed* and transients and had no intention of developing "a great social-work organization," but this did not prevent a sense of partnership with government from pervading the AASW's first delegate assembly in Washington, D.C., in 1934. Representatives from forty-four chapters expressed support for FERA and public works, then went on to urge a permanent federal system with direct relief; they further authorized an ongoing AASW Division on Government and Social Work.

At an APWA event that same year, social workers heard Hopkins affirm the necessity of state public welfare departments to administer outdoor relief and the pensions, but Washington did not give these recipients the priority given the unemployed. Roosevelt did not intend a permanent *federal* "dole," a view shared by other politicians whose commitment to relief extended no further than the current crisis. Within two years, amidst ongoing controversy surrounding several early New Deal initiatives, FERA was dismantled and a new effort, the Works Progress Administration (WPA), was created to provide employment. While many FERA recipients were transferred to WPA work rolls, others again had to seek their essential support from private services, churches, or local general relief.

Having gotten into the politics of FERA's creation, social workers responded angrily to its demise. The director of FWAA developed a point-by-point rebuttal about the inability of the WPA to hire all the "employables" and the inability of private agencies to assist all the "unemployables." Protests were organized against the laying off of FERA staff and the inadequacy of state outdoor relief. When Josephine Brown (1940), Hopkins's assistant, described the end of FERA in *Public Relief, 1929–1939,* she observed that professional social workers had failed to recognize the deep cleavage between their hopes for broad federal relief and the New Deal's commitment to employment as the solution to need.

As FERA's emergency funds were being dispersed, presidential appointees on a Committee on Economic Security began to design *permanent* policies to protect elderly and unemployed workers. During the committee's deliberation, social workers from both public and private organizations were convened for one day in an advisory capacity. Dorothy Kahn, the director of the Philadelphia County Relief Board, who had worked in private family agencies and would be an officer in both AASW and APWA, was appointed chairperson. Those present agreed that the federal government should end "the [state] poor law system of public relief" and establish a "unified welfare program" to include all areas of dependency. Across the nation social workers were writing to legislators in support of these same ideas.

The proposal from the Committee on Economic Security passed in 1935 as the Social Security Act (SSA) contained minimal relief provisions as contrasted to FERA's broad scope. Grants in aid would support extension of existing categorical pensions, to be known as Aid to Dependent Children (ADC), Old-Age Assistance (OAA), and Aid to the Blind (AB). In historic accordance with the protection of states' rights, the bill did not mandate federal determination of administrative standards, eligibility, or benefits; however, eligibility for ADC was narrowed by principles inherent in the previous Mothers' Pension programs. Public workers were to make judgments, often racist, about the suitability of a household receiving relief (Bell, 1965). In the end, states were left to choose whether or not to participate in public assistance (Coll, 1995). Those among the poor who failed to fit into the established categories were bereft of federal protection and left to the vagaries of general relief on a local basis.

Social workers had never spoken unanimously regarding the role of federal government. A few had remained protective of clear lines between public and private roles, but as the depression wore on, those in favor of government became less united as well. At the delegate assembly in 1934, social workers had agreed they had a role in administering federal welfare, but disagreed as to influencing social policy more broadly. In a much discussed speech at the National Conference that year, Mary van Kleeck, a labor and industrial researcher at the Sage Foundation, drew a cheering crowd when she criticized government solutions based on a capitalist economy and recommended shifting power from ownership to labor (Fisher, 1980; Van Kleeck 1934). Those in the loosely organized rank-and-file movement of public welfare workers identified more closely with recipients' rights and collective bargaining than with the training and tasks of graduate social workers in mainline agencies. Between 1933 and 1936, rank-and-file groups claimed more members than AASW, but social workers as a whole were not radicals. Across the country many who had come to welcome federal relief felt that policy questions about restructuring the economy were beyond their professional expertise and they dropped out of the discussion when it reached that point (Bremer, 1984). Among AASW members, some had unabated support for the Roosevelt administration, others had reservations owing in part to the end of FERA and the limitations of the Social Security Act, and a smaller number were deeply dissatisfied with what they believed were Roosevelt's unfulfilled promises.

Participants who headed national social service organizations and most of the social work educational programs agreed generally on reform for adequate relief, but a more radical position was voiced by some in the New York City social welfare community, by people affiliated with the University of Chicago, and by a handful of others for whom reform meant a redistribution of wealth (Leighninger, 1987). As a result of the existing internal disagreements in the social work community and its criticisms of the New Deal, APWA officials announced in 1936 that as an organization they would separate from the National Conference and seek their own professional trajectory (Bremer, 1984).

Social workers generally met Roosevelt's second victory in the 1936 election with less enthusiasm than his first. While New Deal relief continued, the brutal unemployment statistics had lessened, and it seemed clear that innovation in public welfare policy was no longer on the table (Bremer, 1984). For everyone in the profession, the national context for considering relief was changing. The AASW continued its Division on Government and Social Work but its executive director announced in 1937, "The era of considering our job a sort of lobby job in Washington is over" (Leighninger, 1987, p. 67). The director of the FWAA told its membership

> [F]or several years after the beginning of the depression one might justifiably have thought social action was our major concern, at least in practice. Now, however, we are beginning to reexamine our basic reasons for existence as an Association and the ways in which, jointly or individually, we can most effectively define and achieve professional purposes. (Bremer 1984, p. 174)

In a membership survey by FWAA, agencies indicated that "intensive case work," not emergency relief, was their primary function. Sessions at conferences shifted from alarm over the economy to examination of more case-oriented social work (Axinn & Levin, 1975). The obvious policy area open for social workers' professional expertise appeared to be the old one related to standards in the delivery of public relief and the practical issue of whether new public jobs would be filled through patronage and haphazard actions, or by social workers educated and experienced in working with people in distress (Leighninger, 1987). While professional social workers' focus and influence in *determining* public relief policy was limited, their *interpretation* of policy expanded through employment in public relief.

THE DEMAND FOR SOCIAL WORKERS
IN EMERGENCY RELIEF

Although social workers became aware of the limits to their influence in *defining* federal policy in the 1930s, Hopkins recruited them early to shape the *implementation* of FERA by employment in his office and around the country. Members of the APWA were encouraged to help states organize for the delivery of FERA funds. In 1934 Hopkins hired Josephine Brown, a social worker with broad public and private experiences, to head a Social Service Section in Washington. Here social workers were hired to review each state's plan for "intake," the process of receiving applications, establishing eligibility, and determining benefits (Brown, 1940).

Many city governments, including Baltimore, Omaha, Birmingham, and St. Louis, had enlisted private agency personnel to administer their municipal unemployment relief early in the depression. FERA provided a national showcase for continuing such professional efforts. Funds were distributed only through public offices and Hopkins had immediately engaged members of APWA to work in his office and help states organize their emergency programs. However, regulations also required at least one "trained and experienced person" per local emergency relief office, which created jobs for social workers from private agencies.

Incorporating social work expertise into a federal program also meant training *inexperienced* employees. By late 1934, forty thousand employees were administering emergency relief to over four million desperate families. People with some social work credentials supervised unemployed teachers, nurses, and recent college graduates; in rural areas relief employees often lacked education or any experience resembling social work (Brown, 1940; Leighninger, 1987).

Shortly before Hopkins hired her, Brown had authored a text entitled *The Rural Community and Social Case Work* (1933) in which she integrated insights from her own experiences as a farmer and as a county welfare director with the tasks of investigation to determine need. She saw rural areas as having their own particular problems, and as a result she felt that workers needed common sense and a broad understanding of the environment (Davenport & Davenport, 1984). As Hopkins's assistant, Brown drew on her own rural knowledge in designing ways to upgrade the competency of new workers.

In proposing ways to upgrade the skills of new workers Brown clashed with the AASW and graduate social work programs when she offered federal funds to support short-term training institutes to take place at schools, including agricultural colleges, which lacked accredited graduate social work curriculums. The existing graduate social work programs and the professional association conceded to their colleagues and to the reality of the pressing economic challenges. Eventually more than a thousand relief workers who held college degrees received scholarships for graduate work in the existing programs. However, many more personnel participated in state-organized in-service training that Brown encouraged, where content included the practical mechanics of relief administration more than the social or psychological insights characteristic of accredited social work education (Brown, 1940; Leighninger, 1987).

Brown visualized public sector social work as a "democratic" relationship between social workers and recipients, something other than agency casework, monitoring "suitable homes" for mother's pensions, or using new psychological insights to "fix" someone. But Coll (1995) has pointed out that the "means test outlined by FERA for local agencies as a 'minimum investigation' took the identical form followed by leading private agencies" (p. 23). Such case assessment theoretically brought professionalism to the relief enterprise *and* could assure the public that money was spent to the best ends.

"Just" attending to people's financial needs was a challenge. On paper, FERA proposed "Adequacy of Relief" : enough "to prevent physical suffering and maintain minimum living standards whether through wages or direct benefits" (Axinn & Levin, 1975, pp. 198–205). Given the license to determine benefits, Brown found that some relief workers were zealous in safeguarding public coffers, while others sought to equalize wealth. Standards discouraged but did not, in all settings, forbid racial discrimination, meaning that relief workers in both the South and North allocated lesser benefits to African-American families (Coll, 1995). Also, to Brown's regret, she often saw employees more likely to reject than accept applications, although some workers, as in the rank-and-file movement, stood by recipients and carried the demand for assistance to state legislatures.

From the outset, Hopkins had hoped FERA would have a lasting impact on the tradition of stingy relief that marked states' outdoor relief throughout its hundred-plus years existence:

> The first thing for which our money had to go was food to keep people alive. In more places than could be believed, families had been asked to live on two dollars a month. . . . [W]e were able to raise relief to such a sum as fifteen dollars. . . . [W]e must admit that our prevalent standard had no margin of safety. . . . *We have never given adequate relief.* (Brown, 1940, p. 190; emphasis in original)

While FERA only temporarily narrowed the gap between misery and adequacy for thousands of families, its administration provided a less political and more professional model of broad public welfare organization and accountability. This emerged in part from experiences that private agency professionals brought to the short-lived enterprise and its success challenged biases about the potential of the public sector.

SECURING PROFESSIONAL STANDARDS IN PUBLIC ASSISTANCE

Administration of the Social Security Act was lodged within the Social Security Board and Frank Bane of the APWA was the first executive director of operations. Under the auspices of the board, a Bureau of Public Assistance (BPA) was established to monitor the three relief programs. Jane Hoey from New York became the administrator of the BPA and, like Hopkins and Brown before, she plunged into the task of raising administrative standards in public relief.

Since the SSA did not require governors to show "adequate administrative supervision" or "suitable standards of relief," few guarantees existed for the continuation of what professional social workers had applauded as "headway" in public relief standards. Hoey had to find her own ways of working with and around state governments to achieve a public assistance program more consistent and less politicized than the entrenched fiefdoms that had controlled outdoor relief of pensions for mothers, the aged, or blind. She sought the development of local units that would administer the three categorical programs as well as local general relief out of a single office. This type of arrangement was bound to upset existing ad hoc arrangements in rural areas and small towns. This plan also upset social workers in the Children's Bureau, who lobbied unsuccessfully for separate administration and special services for the ADC program (Leighninger, 1987).

An AASW Committee on Standards, Personnel and Service in Public Agencies had asserted earlier that determining public relief eligibility should require no less professional expertise than case assessment in private agencies. Members of the APWA also believed strongly that the quality of public social welfare rested on upgrading personnel (Leighninger, 1987). With this professional consensus, Hoey and others in the federal Social Security apparatus successfully lobbied for legislation in 1939 that mandated states to develop processes for civil service merit exams as a way to challenge the notion that just "anyone" could hand out relief. However, and not surprisingly, state implementation would be slow.

Raising the educational level of public employees would take time; in August 1936 only three states even included education as a qualification for the position of state public assistance director. Public officials were often skeptical about what social work was and why they should support it (Brown, 1940; Patterson, 1981; Leighninger, 1987). When state AASW units offered recommendations for filling public assistance positions, political bias often interfered with alternative suggestions as social workers were seen by many officials as meddling outsiders who misunderstood the exchange of relief and votes.

On the other side of the issue, many social workers in private agencies still rejected public welfare workers as equal professional partners. With the exception of the University of Chicago, where Abbott and Breckinridge emphasized public welfare as a field of professional expertise, curricula in most of the established social work programs continued to focus on casework, with slight attention to public policy and politics. While private agency social workers knew the necessity of *public* relief and spoke of people's "right to assistance," many did not credit employment in that field with the status given social work in other areas and rejected professional association with the low benefits and long waiting lists that characterized many assistance programs (Coll, 1995, Axinn & Levine, 1975).

By the end of the 1930s, the public knew better than before that poverty and the need for assistance was more about economics than character. Public benefits, though still inadequate, were two or three times greater in most locations than had been true a decade earlier. The U.S. census registered a greater increase in social work than any other profession, from 31,000 persons in 1930 to 70,000 in 1940, with tens of thousands more in "semiprofessional" positions. The number of public welfare departments had expanded from several hundred to several thousand with universities opening new schools of social work to meet the demand for trained workers (Fisher, 1980; Wenocur & Reisch, 1989; Coll, 1995). Brown believed that with the New Deal, social work had become an "accepted and established" function of government and part of an expanding public bureaucracy (Brown, 1940, p. 424). The AASW Division on Government and Social Work drafted a statement in 1940 affirming its belief in and support for the "progressive development of public social services," but outlined its continuing concerns as to the "coverage of benefits and the skills of personnel" (NASW/AASW, 1940).

CONCLUSION

This history of relief and social work is full of ironies and contradictions. In spite of American taxpayers' customary resistance to the concept of relief for individual need, the country has consistently provided more aid through taxes than from voluntary donations. While the COS had applauded the demise of municipal relief in the late nineteenth century and in the 1920s and 1930s, voluntary family agencies minimized the impact of financial assistance as a feature of family well-being. Through it all, however, the daily experience of social workers was one of witness to the social, cultural, and personal devastation wrought by poverty. Those same social workers would often work in private agencies that received public funds and would work cooperatively with their counterparts in public relief offices to draw on public relief as a resource for clients.

Prior to the depression, social workers associated with private agencies seemed less concerned with the cruelties of inadequate public benefits than with the flaws of the public sector. They argued that local relief often had more to do with politics than with charity or justice and that, by contrast, professionalism demanded a sound, systematic, scientific, and individual approach independent of political and public control. But by the 1930s, social workers and their organizations had put aside some of these fears and expended great energy in lobbying for public relief. The direction of development in public assistance administration, their increased "socialization," slowly but surely began to counter the decades-long critique that had been lodged in the private sector. Harry Hopkins, Josephine Brown, and Jane Hoey contributed greatly to the diminishment of the private/public disagreement and thousands of unknown social workers acquired a decade of experience testing public and private coordination. However, the old schism was still visible at the end of the decade of the 1930s as professionals in private agencies and social work education would confirm a definition of social work that gave short shrift to public welfare practice.

After World War II, private agencies, the home of standard investigative processes and diverse interventions, lost influence in the public welfare sector and withdrew for a few decades from the major contests over the architecture of public policy. Voluntary family agencies that had "impeded the development of public welfare prior to the depression" would find "a permanent, powerful establishment they could not control" by 1950 (Axinn & Levin, 1975, pp. 192–193).

In the 1950s, states would seek reforms through draconian "suitable home" or "substitute father" provisions. In the 1960s, a combination of social, political, and economic influences pushed into being a larger set of reform social policy. Tools other than relief were created; community-based programs initiated by the Office of Economic Opportunity often relied on non–social work staff. Federal courts and federal policy in the 1960s ended welfare workers' authority in denying ADC owing to a negative assessment about family life. Major amendments to the Social Security Act in 1962 and 1967 encouraged and supported public welfare agencies to expand their services with the goal of "rehabilitation" (self-sufficiency) for relief recipients. Wilbur J. Cohen, "Mr. Social Security" owing to his decades of employment in federal social welfare and role as secretary of Health, Education, and Welfare during the Johnson administration, observed that professional social workers had not been "automatic allies" in developing welfare policy and that public welfare still lacked "status" in social work (Berkowitz, 1995).

Social work would not be a reliable ally and would not grant public welfare work status because of a persistent idea: a profession that would *not be defined* by poverty or the poor and a profession that would have a methodology and practice as applicable in mental health or hospital social work as in child welfare or ADC. This dream of a social work practice and a profession modeled after medicine would be compelling and controlling and it would shape both social work's reluctance to embrace public welfare and its ultimate alienation from public policy related to poverty.

REFERENCES

Abramovitz, M. (1996). *Regulating the Lives of Women: Social Welfare Policy from Colonial Times to the Present* (rev. ed.). Boston: South End Press.

Axinn, J., & Levin, H. (1975). *Social Welfare: A History of the American Response to Need.* New York: Dodd, Mead.

Bell, W. (1965). *Aid to Dependent Children.* New York: Columbia University Press.

Berkowitz, E. D. (1995). *Mr. Social Security: The Life of Wilbur J. Cohen.* Lawrence: University of Kansas Press.

Bremer, W. (1984). *Depression Winters: New York Social Workers and the New Deal.* Philadelphia: Temple University Press.

Bremner, R. H. (Ed.) (1971). *Children and Youth in America: A Documentary History* (Vol. 2). Cambridge, MA: Harvard University Press.

Brock, W. R. (1984). *Investigation and Responsibility: Public Responsibility in the United States, 1865–1900*. New York: Cambridge University Press.

Brown, J. C. (1933). *The Rural Community and Social Case Work*. New York: Family Welfare Association of New York.

Brown, J. C. (1940). *Public Relief, 1929–1939*. New York: Holt, Rinehart, & Wilson. (Reprinted, 1971, New York: Octagon Books.)

Colcord, J. C. (1930). Facing the coming winter. *Survey, 65*, 206–208.

Coll, B. (1995). *Safety Net: Welfare and Social Security, 1929–1979*. New Brunswick, NJ: Rutgers University Press.

Committee on Families and Neighborhoods (1912). Report of the committee on families and neighborhoods with the committee on children. In *Proceedings* (pp. 468–498). Chicago: University of Chicago Press.

Costin, L. B. (1983). *Two Sisters for Social Justice: A Biography of Grace and Edith Abbott*. Urbana: University of Illinois Press.

Davenport, J., & Davenport, J. (1984). Josephine brown's classic book still guides rural social work. *Social Casework, 65* (7), 413–419.

Devine, E. (1905). *The Principles of Relief*. New York: MacMillan

Fisher, J. (1980). *The Response of Social Work to the Depression*. Boston: G. K. Hall.

Geddes, A. E. (1937). *Trends in Relief Expenditures, 1910–1935*. Research monograph of the Works Progress Administration. Washington, DC: Government Printing Office.

Hamilton, G. (1931). Refocusing family case work. *Proceedings of the National Conference of Social Work* (pp. 170–188). Chicago: University of Chicago Press.

Hopkins, H. L. (1933). The developing national program of relief. *Proceedings of the National Conference of Social Work* (pp. 65–71) Chicago: U. of Chicago Press.

Katz, M. (1986). *In the Shadow of the Poorhouse: A Social History of Welfare in America*. New York: Basic Books.

Ladd-Taylor, M. (1994). *Mother-Work: Women, Child Welfare and the State, 1890–1930*. Urbana: University of Illinois Press.

Leff, M. H. (1973). Consensus for reform: the mothers' pension movement in the progressive era. *Social Services Review, 47*, 397–417.

Leighninger, L. (1987). *Social Work—Search for Identity*. Westport, CT: Greenwood.

Lowell, J. S. ([1884] 1971). *Private Charity and Public Relief*. New York: Arno (reprint of the original).

Lubove, R. (1965). *The Professional Altruist: The Emergence of Social Work as a Career 1880–1930*. Cambridge, MA: Harvard University Press.

Lubove, R. (1968). *The Struggle for Social Security, 1900–1935* . Cambridge, MA: Harvard University Press.

Muncy, R. (1991). *Creating a Female Dominion in American Reform, 1890–1935*. New York: Oxford University Press.

NASW/AASW (1940). Statement of AASW position on public welfare services. Box 19, Folder 211. Social Welfare History Archives, University of Minnesota Libraries.

Patterson, J. T. (1981). *America's Struggle against Poverty, 1900–1980*. Cambridge, MA: Harvard University Press.

Pumphrey, M. W., & Pumphrey, R. E. (1983). The widow's pension movement, 1900–1930: Preventive child saving or social control. In Walter I. Trattner (Ed.), *Social Welfare or Social Control? Some Reflections on Regulating the Poor* (pp. 52–54) Knoxville: University of Tennessee.

Richmond, M. (1913). Motherhood and pensions. *Survey, 29,* 774–780.

Scott, A. F. (1990). Women's voluntary associations: From charity to reform. In D. McCarthy (Ed.), *Lady Bountiful Revisited: Women, Philanthropy Power.* New Brunswick, NJ: Rutgers University Press.

Skocpol, T. (1992). *Protecting Soldiers and Mothers: The Political Origins of Social Policy in the United States.* Cambridge, MA: Harvard University. Press.

Springer, G. (1931). The challenge of hard times. *Survey, 66,* 380–385.

Trattner, W. I. (1994). *From Poor Law to Welfare State: A History of Social Welfare in America* (5th ed.). New York: Free Press.

Van Kleeck, M. (1934). Common goals of labor and social work. In *Proceedings* (pp. 285–303). Chicago: University of Chicago Press.

Walker, S. H. (1933). Privately supported social work: President's research committee on social trends. In *Recent Social Trends in the United States* (Vol. 2, pp. 1168–1170). New York: McGraw-Hill.

Warner, A. G. (1894). *American Charities.* New York: Crowell. (Reprinted, 1989, New Brunswick, NJ: Transaction.)

Watson, F. D. ([1922] 1971). *The Charity Organization Movement in the United States: A Study in American Philanthropy.* New York: Arno (reprint of the original).

Wenocur, S., & Reisch, M. (1989). *From Charity to Enterprise: The Development of Social Work in a Market Economy.* Urbana: University of Illinois Press.

4

"In a World Gone Industrial"
Specialization and the Search for Social Work Practice above the Poverty Line[1]

PAUL H. STUART

The question of social work's disengagement from the poor has been raised since at least 1930, when social reformer A. J. Muste complained that family agencies "have gone psychiatric in a world which has gone industrial" (quoted in Ross & Kellogg, 1930, p. 344). Not surprisingly, the existence of social work's disengagement from the poor, or at least of its undesirability, has been a subject of dispute. Even when the phenomenon is admitted, explanations have similarly been a source of some controversy.

In 1994, Harry Specht and Mark Courtney published *Unfaithful Angels*, subtitled *How Social Work Has Abandoned Its Mission*. They argued that "social work has abandoned its mission to help the poor and oppressed and to build communality" across classes (p. 4). They criticized social workers for embracing the "popular psychotherapies" and for pursuing the lure of private practice, which they suggested was motivated by a desire "to obtain more autonomy over their practice and to earn more money" (p. 126). Social workers' attachment to private practice and the profession's infatuation with the popular psychotherapies had resulted in its abandonment of the public social services that assisted the poor, according to Specht and Courtney. Social work had been founded by pioneers like Jane Addams and Mary Richmond who had "a vision of a profession that would help construct the city on the hill . . . instead at this century's end, we have a profession dedicated to building the church of individual repair" (p. 85).

Specht and Courtney are the latest in a series of critics who have complained about social work's disengagement from the poor. Among the explanations advanced since the 1920s have been the following:

- In 1929, in his presidential address to the National Conference of Social Work, Porter Lee declared that social work, "once a cause," was now a "function of a well-ordered society." The reasons for the change from cause to function were many, but boiled down to the institutionalization of social services, an increasing public recognition of their importance and a belief that the social services were essential for the operation of a well-ordered society. The danger of social work as function, according to Lee, was that social workers might lose all sense of cause and be content to serve merely as functionaries in an increasingly organized society.
- In the 1950s, both Herbert Bisno (1956) and Ernest Greenwood (1957) suggested that the effort to gain professional acceptance and status had diverted social work from its mission to serve the poor and accomplish social change.
- In the 1960s, Richard Cloward and Irwin Epstein (1965) suggested that the creation of public welfare programs during the Great Depression of the 1930s and their subsequent expansion in the intervening decades had enabled family adjustment agencies to shift their function from giving relief to the poor to providing counseling services to an increasingly middle-class clientele.
- In the 1970s and 1980s, many observers attributed social work's disengagement from the poor to the deterioration of public social services—and the government's shift in funding, which favored "hard" services more than "soft" services like counseling—and the attractions of private and other for-profit forms of practice, which promised more personal satisfaction and income to social workers (Jayaratne, Davis-Sacks, & Chess, 1991).

The suggestion in all of these is that the development of social work specialization, and specifically psychiatric social work, had a significant impact on the profession's commitment to the poor.

However, rather than a development unique to social work, the trend toward increased specialization has been noted in a number of twentieth-century professions and organizations. Specialization is a characteristic of contemporary formal and professional organization (Raelin, 1986). Indeed, leaders in the social work profession self-consciously adopted a model of professionalization that was consistent with the developing image of professions in twentieth-century American society. Consistent with an increasing rationalization of work and the domination of the society by formal organizations, this model resulted in the increased rationalization of professional functions and increased intraprofessional specialization.

Evaluating the Specht and Courtney critique, and similar critiques, may tell us much about the causes and extent of social work's disengagement from the poor, the influence of social work specializations, and the history of the social work profession. This chapter will examine the coexistence of generalist and specialized social work practice before World War I, the dominance of specialized practice in the 1920s, and the influence of specializations on practice.

EARLY GENERIC AND SPECIALIZED SOCIAL WORK PRACTICE

Before World War I, "general practice" in social work meant practice in the Charity Organization Societies (COS) and the settlement house movement. Both kinds of agencies self-consciously viewed themselves as the true "general practitioners" in social work and, indeed, some of the rivalry between the two movements may have resulted from these self-images. Under the leadership of Mary Richmond, the COSs were rapidly developing a family treatment technique that would become known as social case work. In 1909, Richmond became director of the Charity Organization Department of the Russell Sage Foundation, a position that gave her time to research and the power to allocate funds to change local COSs. The emerging social case work technique was sociological rather than psychological since Richmond emphasized environmental factors in social diagnosis and their manipulation in social treatment. The Russell Sage Foundation, in turn, supported the development of a national standard-setting organization, led by Richmond and Francis McLean, another Russell Sage Foundation staff member, called the American Association for Organizing Charity, which would later become the Family Service Association of America.

Settlement houses, more eclectic in method, used the neighborhood as the focus of effort and pioneered a variety of social service and state regulatory social welfare programs based on discovered neighborhood needs (Addams, 1930). Located largely in immigrant districts of large and middle-sized American cities, settlement houses often emphasized the recreational needs of their poor and working-class neighbors. They became leaders in providing recreational and group opportunities to children, youth, and adults in American cities.

In addition to settlement houses and COSs, a variety of specialized fields of practice were introduced prior to World War I:

- hospital social work (begun at Massachusetts General Hospital in 1905)
- school social work (begun in Hartford, Connecticut, in 1906)
- psychiatric social work (begun at Massachusetts General Hospital in 1907)

- in addition, a variety of nineteenth-century child-saving activities were coalescing into the field of child welfare during the first decades of the twentieth century (Costin, Karger, & Stoesz, 1996).

In school, hospital, and psychiatric social work, practice was sociological rather than psychological in nature. The focus of practitioners was on the "here and now" (Stuart, 1997) as it was in contemporary charity organization and child welfare work. Social workers in these specializations emphasized the investigation and manipulation of environmental factors. In the words of an early visiting teacher, as school social workers were known, the function of visiting teachers was "socializing the school and individualizing the child" (quoted in Lubove, 1965, p. 37). In 1916, school social workers in twelve cities devoted most of their attention to "interpreting to the school the child's out-of-school life" and "interpreting to the parent the demands of the school" (Culbert, 1916, p. 595). As observers of social work practice from Abraham Flexner (1915) to William Schwartz (1969) have observed, social workers had an essentially mediating function.

Psychiatric social work began as a part of the movement for community care of the mentally ill in the early twentieth century. Psychiatrists became interested in securing community placement for hospitalized psychiatric patients and averting hospitalization for some new patients. However, nothing in their training or skills prepared them for community work. Social workers provided much-needed knowledge of the community, gathering facts about the patient's home environment, supervising community placements, securing lodging and employment, and connecting the patient with needed community services (Stuart, 1997).

The relationship between generalist and specialized social work was a thorny one. In 1910, Mary Richmond attempted to develop a model for a relationship between the COSs and the various specialized movements then existing within social work. She saw the COS as a local clearinghouse for national reform movements. The COS worker would gather information needed by the reform movement and in turn would receive information as to how to approach social problems identified by the various reform movements (Richmond, 1910b).

Richmond organized a panel on the "Inter-Relation of Social Movements" at the 1910 National Conference of Charities and Correction and had the Russell Sage Foundation produce a pamphlet with the same title (Richmond, 1910a). However, Richmond's efforts did not result in recognition of the central role of the COSs. They were in competition with settlement houses. The settlements often had stronger connections with reform movements than COSs. In addition, the COSs often had a strained relationship with child welfare agencies over the issue of which was to be the central or primary agency to work with children in families (Costin, Karger, & Stoesz, 1996).

At the end of World War I, social work, including its specializations and general practice branches, was poised for new departures. At the 1919 National Conference of Social Work, three papers on psychiatric social work created a stir (Robinson, 1930). Mary Jarrett (1919), the leading psychiatric social worker of her day, argued that psychiatry, along with economics and biology, provided a necessary scientific basis for contemporary social work. However, psychiatric social work was not different from social work in other fields, Jarrett argued, except in that it was practiced in a psychiatric setting. Jessie Taft (1919) contradicted Jarrett, calling for raising standards of training and practice for psychiatric social workers. Taft complained that much psychiatric social work was "just ordinary social service which only happens to be directed toward the mentally ill" (p. 593). In a third paper, E. E. Southard (1919), a psychiatrist and Jarrett's erstwhile superior at Massachusetts Psychopathic Hospital, objected to the prevailing emphasis on the family in Mary Richmond's social case work. Since family dysfunction was usually traceable to the influence of one troubled family member, Southard said, the individual was a much more promising focus for the profession.[2]

During the 1920s, the school and psychiatric specializations expanded as a result of investments of resources by the Commonwealth Fund. Founded in 1918, the fund initiated a program to combat juvenile delinquency as a way to influence the development of the child welfare specialization in social work. The fund made major investments in school social work and child guidance clinics and supported expanded educational programs for the preparation of psychiatric and school social workers. These efforts stimulated the development of the two specializations, and contributed to the eventual development of a psychological orientation in child welfare work.

SPECIALIZED PRACTICE IN THE 1920s AND AFTER

During the decade of the 1920s, specialized practice replaced generalist practice in social work. The two generalist settings, COSs and settlement houses, were largely transformed into specialized agencies. The American Association for Organizing Charity changed its name to the American Association for Organizing Family Social Work in 1919 and helped COSs make the transition to family welfare agencies (Kempton, 1919). Contributing to this change were the American Red Cross's experiments with "case work above the poverty line" during World War I. The Red Cross Home Service provided social case work services to families of armed services personnel. Mary Richmond, whose influential *Social Diagnosis* (1917) was followed by *What Is Social Case Work?* (1922), was actively involved in training the Red Cross Home Service workers. The new family service focus resulted in a growing conviction that family social workers should work with "all groups in the community," and not only those in economic crisis (Taussig, 1926, p. 286). The American Association for Organizing Family Social Work became the Family Welfare Association of America in 1930 and in 1946 changed its name again, to the Family Service Association of America.

Settlement houses developed a specialized practice orientation as well. By the late 1920s, settlements were specializing in providing recreational services to economically diverse groups of neighborhood children and youth (Stuart, 1990). The National Federation of Settlements, a national standard-setting organization, actively assisted settlement houses develop their recreation programs. Later in the decade, when the growth of city recreation departments threatened to make recreation a local government activity, removing what had become the raison d'etre for many settlements, the National Federation began to promote adult education as a new focus for settlement houses. In some settlements that were located in neighborhoods where considerable out-migration had occurred, the majority of participants in settlement programs were former neighbors, now middle- class suburbanites, who returned to the old neighborhood to participate in settlement activities (Stuart, 1992).

The increasing specialization of former settings for general practice, family service agencies and settlement houses, resulted in part from dynamics internal to the respective fields. The external environment, especially the funding environment of voluntary social services, also had an effect. During the 1920s, a federated fund-raising organization, the Community Chest, became the predominant means of financing voluntary social services, including family agencies and settlements, in most cities. Reliance on the Community Chest resulted in "stereotyped forms of social work," in the words of one settlement house leader (Cooper, 1923, p. 24), because of the way in which the chests allocated funds to member agencies. The Community Chests divided agencies into functional fields, such as family case work, group work, and health, and allocated funds to agencies within those specialized fields of social agency function. Thus, participating in the Community Chest caused agencies to focus on a particular kind of service for which a demonstrable need existed. The participating agency justified its annual budget request on the basis of the provision of a service that met an identifiable community need. Settlements were usually placed in the local chest's group work council and received funds based upon their provision of group work and recreational services. Family agencies increasingly concentrated on family case work, especially when public relief programs were expanded during the Great Depression of the 1930s (Cloward & Epstein, 1965). In effect, the expansion of public relief removed the provision of relief from the family agency's domain. By the end of the depression, the Family Welfare Association of America had a committee on marriage counseling in family agencies. Significantly, fee-charging was one of the issues the committee addressed, suggesting that the introduction of marriage counseling resulted in increased service to the nonpoor (Family Welfare Association of America, 1943).

By the early 1940s then, several significant specializations in social work had begun to serve clients who were not poor and to construe social work practice as applicable across the social spectrum. If many of the clients of social workers were still relatively poor people, the process of specialization had resulted in a refocusing of the social worker's attention on characteristics other than the client's poverty. This trend toward specialization was not something that satisfied all social workers. Much of the motivation for the 1929 Milford Conference Report, *Social Case Work: Generic and Specific,* was the discomfort of agency leaders with the increasingly specialized nature of practice. The report concluded that social case work had a generic core that could be applied in a variety of specialized settings, none of them poverty specific. Twenty years later, Helen Harris Perlman (1949) decried the lack of progress toward generic progress since the Milford Conference Report: "The search for generic aspects among the specific settings," she wrote, "may serve in a small way to expand and deepen our base of professional unity" (p. 301).

In 1955, the social work profession attempted to deepen its base of professional unity in a significant way. In that year, the American Association of Social Workers joined with six specialized professional associations to form the National Association of Social Workers (NASW). Over the next decade, NASW moved to remove the vestiges of the specialized predecessor organizations from its structure (Stuart, 1986). In addition, the association established a Commission on Social Work Practice, chaired by medical social worker Harriet Bartlett, which developed a "Working Definition of Social Work Practice" (Bartlett, 1958; Gordon, 1962). In spite of the development of a variety of "generalist" practice theories, reflected in widely used social work practice textbooks in the 1970s (Payne, 1991), specializations continued to be strong in social work. Responding to the growth of external specialized professional associations, NASW by the mid-1980s was strengthening its specialization-oriented activities (Stuart, 1986).

SPECIALIZATIONS AND DISENGAGEMENT FROM THE POOR

Many of the activities of NASW since its inception, including the effort to develop a working definition of social work practice and the reorganizations of the 1960s, was predicated on a unitary model of professional development. A unified profession was like a community, according to this view. It was thought that overattention to specialized practice concerns would weaken social work by diverting the profession from its central tasks.

An alternative view of professions, the process model developed by sociologists Rue Bucher and Anselm Strauss (1961), views professions as loose amalgamations of specializations that are in competition with one another for resources. Arenas for conflict include professional schools where new professionals are socialized, external funding sources, and referral sources. Specializations that interact with nonmembers of the profession may be strengthened by virtue of their access to funding sources, clients, or other resources. Several writers have found the model to be applicable to social work (Carlton, 1977; Leighninger, 1987; Stuart, 1986).

Divisions within firms or other organizations that span the boundaries that separate firms from their environments may influence other components of the organization. Such components as sales, marketing, and financing departments in firms are responsible for securing resources for the organization from external sources. Boundary spanners are thought to be powerful within organizations because their access to needed resources commands attention (Thompson, 1967). Specializations in social work often had a boundary-spanning function. During the 1920s, the availability of training and program funds from the Commonwealth Fund for psychiatric and school social work greatly enhanced the viability of those specializations, and of the social work profession as a whole. After World War II, the availability of federal funding for psychiatric social work fostered the expansion of this specialization, continuing the work begun by the Commonwealth Fund in the 1920s.

As noted above, goal displacement is often found to be a problem for social workers in secondary settings (Klein, 1959; Bartlett, 1954). Even in the so-called "primary settings," settings where social work is the primary profession, goal displacement may present difficulties. Each setting for specialized practice has what Harriet Bartlett (1954) called a unique social objective. In an elaboration of the field of practice concept of specialization, Elliot Studt (1965) referred to the "social task" of a field of practice. The social task of the corrections field was identified by Studt as "moral functioning" (p. 160).

The concept of a specialization's social objective or social task may help to explain social work's disengagement from poverty as a public issue, if not from the poor. Early psychiatric social workers, like social workers in other professions, practiced mostly with poor people. Yet their social objective was not the eradication of poverty, as it was for the settlement house and charity organization workers, but mental hygiene, defined as the prevention and amelioration of mental illness. Similarly, in the 1920s, when charity workers became family social workers and settlement houses became recreation centers, few social workers remained whose central objective was the eradication of poverty. Significantly, the settlement houses that took the lead in social action during the 1930s were located in New York and Chicago. These settlements were not pressured to specialize in the provision of recreational services because their cities did not develop federated fund-raising programs until the middle of the decade (Trolander, 1975).

It was not psychiatric social workers alone who began to practice "above the poverty line" in the 1920s and 1930s. Like the psychiatric social workers, hospital, school, family, and settlement house social workers encountered working- and middle-class clients as they focused on social objectives that affected the nonpoor and as their services became institutionalized in American cities. Both internal and external factors may explain the growth of specialization in social work, but specialization itself, because it focused the attention of social workers on problems other than poverty, explains social work's disengagement from the poor.

In conclusion, the rise of psychiatric social work does not explain social work's disengagement from the poor as some critics contend. Psychiatric social workers were not the only social workers, or even the first, to practice "above the poverty line" during World War I and after. Nor was psychiatric social work the only or even the first field of practice to develop social work treatment methods that appealed to working- and even middle-class clients. The recreation programs of the settlements and the marriage counseling programs of the family agencies were developed prior to client-centered counseling and the popular psychotherapies. Social work's origins were in late nineteenth-century campaigns to help the poor and eradicate poverty. Social work's general practitioners, the settlement houses and the COSs, carried those campaigns into the early twentieth century. Unfortunately, when the former general practitioners became specialists during the 1920s, no one was left to campaign for the poor.

NOTES

1. An earlier version of this chapter was presented at a faculty colloquium at the School of Social Work, University of Alabama. I would like to thank Joan E. Esser-Stuart and Ginny T. Raymond for helpful comments on an earlier draft of the paper.

2. A year earlier, Southard (1918) had reanalyzed the cases presented by Mary Richmond in her classic *Social Diagnosis* (1917). Southard's analysis showed, to his satisfaction, that most of the clients discussed by Richmond were suffering from psychiatric problems.

REFERENCES

Addams, J. (1930). Social workers and the other professions. In *Proceedings of the National Conference of Social Work, 57*, 50–54.

Bartlett, H. M. (1954). The influence of setting on social work practice. In *Social Work Practice in the Medical and Psychiatric Setting, Institute Proceedings, 1951. School of Social Work, University of Pittsburgh* (pp. 11–26). Pittsburgh: University of Pittsburgh Press.

Bartlett, H. M. (1958). Toward clarification and improvement of social work practice. *Social Work, 3*(2), 3–9.

Bisno, H. (1956). How social will social work be? *Social Work, 1*(2), 12–18.

Bucher, R., & Strauss, A. (1961). Professions in process. *American Journal of Sociology, 66,* 325–334.

Carlton, T. O. (1977). Social work as a profession in process. *Journal of Social Welfare, 4,* 15–25.

Cloward, R. A., & Epstein, I. (1965). Private social welfare's disengagement from the poor: The case of family adjustment agencies. In M. N. Zald (Ed.), *Social Welfare Institutions* (pp. 623–644). New York: Wiley.

Cooper, C. C. (1923). *Settlement Finance.* Boston: National Federation of Settlements.

Costin, L. B., Karger, H. J., & Stoesz, D. (1996). *The Politics of Child Abuse in America.* New York: Oxford University Press.

Culbert, J. (1916). Visiting teachers and their activities. In *Proceedings of the National Conference of Charities and Corrections, 43,* 592–598.

Family Welfare Association of America (1943). *Report of the Committee on Marriage Counseling.* Records of the Family Service Association of America, Box 10. Social Welfare History Archives, University of Minnesota Libraries.

Flexner, A. (1915). Is social work a profession? *Proceedings of the National Conference of Charities and Corrections* (pp. 576–590). Baltimore, MD: Russell Sage Foundation.

Gordon, W. E. (1962). A critique of the working definition. *Social Work, 7*(4), 3–13.

Greenwood, E. (1957). Attributes of a Profession. *Social Work, 2*(3), 45–55.

Jarrett, M. (1919). The psychiatric thread running through all social case work. *Proceedings of the National Conference of Social Work, 46,* 587–593.

Jayaratne, S., Davis-Sacks, M. L., & Chess, W. (1991). Private practice may be good for your health and well-being. *Social Work, 36,* 224–229.

Kempton, H. P. (1919). Family social work. *Survey, 42*(June 21), 468–469.

Klein, A. F. (1959). Social work in non-social work settings. *Social Work, 4*(4), 92–97.

Lee, P. R. (1929). Social work: Cause and function. *Proceedings of the National Conference of Social Work, 56,* 3–20.

Leighninger, L. (1987). *Social Work: Search for Identity.* Westport, CT: Greenwood.

Lubove, R. (1965). *The Professional Altruist: The Emergence of Social Work as a Career, 1880–1930.* Cambridge, MA: Harvard University Press.

Milford Conference (1929). *Social Case Work: Generic and Specific.* New York: American Association of Social Workers.

Payne, M. (1991). *Modern Social Work Theory: A Critical Introduction.* Chicago: Lyceum.

Perlman, H. H. (1949). Generic aspects of specific case-work settings. *Social Service Review, 23,* 293–301.

Raelin J. A. (1986). *The Clash of Cultures: Managers and Professionals.* Boston: Harvard Business School Press.

Richmond, M. (1910a). *The Inter-Relation of Social Movements with Information about Sixty-Seven Organizations.* New York: Russell Sage Foundation.

Richmond, M. (1910b). Report of the committee: The inter-relation of social movements. *Proceedings of the National Conference of Charities and Correction, 37,* 212–218.

Richmond, M. (1917). *Social Diagnosis.* New York: Russell Sage Foundation.

Richmond, M. (1922). *What Is Social Case Work?* New York: Russell Sage Foundation.

Robinson, V. P. (1930). *A Changing Psychology in Social Case Work.* Chapel Hill: University of North Carolina Press.

Ross, M., & Kellogg, P. U. (1930). New beacons in Boston: The fifty-seventh National Conference of Social Work. *Survey, 64,* 341–347, 361, 367.

Schwartz, W. (1969). Private troubles and public issues: One social work job or two? *Social Welfare Forum, 96,* 22–43.

Southard, E. E. (1918). The kingdom of evil: Advantages of an orderly approach in social case analysis. *Proceedings of the National Conference of Social Work, 45,* 334–340.

Southard, E. E. (1919). The individual versus the family as the unit of interest in social work. *Proceedings of the National Conference of Social Work, 46,* 582–587.

Specht, H., & Courtney, M. (1994). *Unfaithful Angels: How Social Work Has Abandoned Its Mission.* New York: Free Press.

Stuart, P. H. (1986). School social work as a professional segment: Continuity in transitional times. *Social Work in Education, 8,* 141–153.

Stuart, P. H. (1990). Settlement houses: Changing sources of innovation in social work. In H. H. Weissman (Ed.), *Serious Play: Creativity and Innovation in Social Work* (pp. 198–208). Silver Spring, MD: National Association of Social Workers.

Stuart, P. H. (1992). Philanthropy, voluntarism, and innovation: Settlement houses in twentieth-century America. *Essays in Philanthropy, No. 5.* Indianapolis: Indiana University Center on Philanthropy.

Stuart, P. H. (1997). Community care and the origins of psychiatric social work. *Social Work in Health Care, 25*(3), 25–36.

Studt, E. (1965). Fields of social work practice: Organizing our resources for more effective practice. *Social Work, 10*(4), 156–165.

Taft, J. (1919). Qualifications of the psychiatric social worker. *Proceedings of the National Conference of Social Work, 46,* 593–599.

Taussig, F. (1926). Widening horizons in family case work. *Family, 6,* 283–286.

Thompson, J. D. (1967). *Organizations in Action.* New York: McGraw-Hill.

Trolander, J. A. (1975). *Settlement Houses and the Great Depression.* Detroit: Wayne State University Press.

5

The Service Trap
Social Work and Public Welfare Policy in the 1960s

LESLIE LEIGHNINGER

> The very essence of a vital [public welfare] program should be the full use of all rehabilitative services. . . . The ultimate aim is to help families to become self-supporting and independent by strengthening all their own resources. Achieving this requires the special knowledge and skill of social workers with graduate training
>
> Ad Hoc Committee on Public Welfare, *Recommendations for Public Welfare Reorganization*

At the beginning of the 1960s, social work was poised to make its greatest contribution yet to the development of public welfare policy and programs in the United States. The creation of the 1962 Social Security Amendments (the "service amendments") was perhaps the apex of social work influence on federal social policymaking. Yet by the latter part of the decade other measures rivaled the services approach; social workers no longer held the attention of federal welfare officials; and the goal of a highly professionalized, casework-oriented public welfare system seemed increasingly irrelevant to critics both to the left and the right of the political spectrum. Although social workers had fulfilled one of their missions—large-scale federal support for social work education—this achievement may have served more to sustain a narrow professionalism than to meet the needs of the poor.

Social work is often criticized for its stress on professionalization and its lack of attention to the causes and effects of poverty (see, e.g., Wenocur & Reisch, 1989; Ehrenreich, 1985; Specht and Courtney, 1994), but is the description of the profession in the 1960s simply a story of social workers fixated on a casework-based welfare system that promoted their own interests at the expense of those of the poor? Did their loss of influence stem from the failure of services to deliver promised results? I will argue that the picture is much more complex. Social workers were not alone in their promotion of services. Nor was this their only suggestion for dealing with poverty. Professional concerns competed with broader visions, producing conflicting goals. The profession's program and strategies, its successes and failures, were affected not only by forces internal to the profession, but by the economic and political context of the times.

The 1962 amendments, and social work's involvement in their passage, were influenced by a variety of developments in the 1950s. These included a growing backlash against public welfare, especially the Aid To Dependent Children (ADC) program; the promotion of particular initiatives by the Bureau of Public Assistance (the federal department responsible for ADC); and the development of social action commitments and activities by social work and social welfare organizations.

Attacks on public welfare took place throughout the 1950s. They were prompted in part by a rise in welfare costs that stemmed from inflation and the expansion of benefits. In addition, the fact that Social Security had taken over coverage of "respectable" widows and children of insured workers meant that "less desirable" clients—African-American families and illegitimate children—were becoming more prominent in the ADC caseload (a large percentage of African-American men worked as farm laborers, an occupation not covered by Social Security until 1954). Charges of welfare fraud took place in many communities, and social workers were sometimes blamed for contributing to the abuse of public funds. Racist attitudes linked African-American women with laziness and immorality. Illegitimacy was viewed as a major cause of welfare dependency, and a number of states began to develop laws and policies that would exclude illegitimate children from the coverage. The 1950s also witnessed the onset of the infamous "midnight raids," or unannounced visits to uncover the presence of "unauthorized men" in recipients' homes (Bell, 1965; Coll, 1995). In 1961, a study of public assistance noted that ADC had become "one of the most controversial and misunderstood programs in the United States" (quoted in Bell, 1965, p. 75).

The Bureau of Public Assistance often acted cautiously in responding to attacks on ADC and to states' efforts to restrict coverage of children born out of wedlock (Coll, 1995; Bell, 1965). Reflecting the federal system of American government and the strength of states' rights, the Social Security Act had given states a good deal of discretion in running their public assistance programs. This limited BPA's power. One response of the federal bureau, however, was to call for an increase in social services to deal with such problems as illegitimacy and dependency in ADC families. This idea had been around for some time, both within and outside BPA. The notion of individualized services—advice, information, and casework—offered by trained social workers had been suggested by Elizabeth Wickenden as early as 1949. Wickenden, an expert in social policy, spoke on behalf of the American Public Welfare Association (APWA), an influential organization of state public welfare administrators and other welfare officials.

The services stress was greatly bolstered by the appointment of Charles Schottland as commissioner of Social Security in 1954. Schottland, a former public welfare administrator and Children's Bureau staff member, was sympathetic to social workers and believed that social services could play an important role in public welfare agencies. Supporting BPA's interest in legitimizing the place of services in ADC, Schottland helped win acceptance of a services provision in the 1956 amendments to the Social Security Act. This measure encouraged states to furnish "rehabilitation and other services . . . to needy dependent children and the parents or relatives with whom they are living to help maintain and strengthen family life" and to promote self-support and independence (Coll, 1995, p. 195; Schottland, 1965).

The mechanism for encouraging states to follow the new directive was a federal match for the cost of providing services. However, the law did not require states to offer services, and Congress subsequently declined to make the necessary appropriations. The services idea had thus been legitimized as a public welfare function, but its centrality to that function was not yet established.

Although vaguely defined, the services envisioned by BPA, Schottland, and APWA were to be delivered primarily by professionally trained social workers. The 1956 amendments included an authorization to appropriate funds for training although, again, no appropriation was made. BPA had long promoted professional education for social workers in state and local welfare departments, and had supported the use of ADC administrative funds for paid work release programs that allowed welfare workers to attend graduate school. The proportion of MSWs in public welfare had always been small; in 1960 only 13 percent of supervisors and 1 percent of caseworkers held graduate social work degrees (Bell, 1965). The emphasis on social services provided a new opportunity for BPA to call for federally funded professional training of employees.

The BPA was staffed largely by trained social workers, and welfare historian Blanche Coll (1995) notes their leadership in shaping public assistance policy. But BPA staff did not necessarily speak for all of professional social work. The two major professional organizations, the National Association of Social Workers (NASW) and the Council on Social Work Education (CSWE) represented broad constituencies within the field. Each group articulated a variety of positions regarding public welfare, staffing and training issues, and the role of social workers in lobbying and other forms of social action.

Both NASW and CSWE were new organizations in the 1950s. Each inherited certain policies and commitments from predecessor groups. The organizing committee representing the seven groups that formed NASW, for example, affirmed "the importance of social action as a part of the social work function." The committee set up a Commission on Social Policy and Action that was incorporated into the new organization upon its formation in 1955. The commission's immediate work was to examine issues related to the developing federal health and welfare programs. The organizing committee also recommended the continuation of a Washington office set up by one of the predecessor organizations in 1953. The functions of this office had been to report on federal developments in social work and to carry on lobbying activities (Anderson, 1955). The new association voted to maintain the office and included in the NASW bylaws the objective of "alleviating or preventing sources of deprivation, distress, and strain susceptible of being influenced by social work methods and by social action" (NASW, 1959, p. 4).

Together the Washington office and the Commission on Social Policy and Action carried out three types of activities: liaison work with representatives of federal agencies and other organizations with a social welfare interest, lobbying and congressional testimony, and aid to chapters in dealing with state and local legislative issues. The work of the new commission met with Schottland's approval. He contrasted their approach with that of the earlier American Association of Social Workers (AASW), a group he saw as private agency–dominated and "very suspicious of public services." The AASW had rejected Schottland's suggestion of an advisory committee to HEW on social work matters; in contrast, the NASW's HEW Liaison Committee conferred with the secretary of the department, the commissioner of Social Security, and the heads of HEW Bureaus (NASW, 1959; Schottland, 1965, pp. 65–66).

Yet as an organization primarily of social work practitioners, NASW sometimes had trouble justifying and sustaining its social action strategies and goals. At a meeting of a committee evaluating the work of the Commission on Social Policy, one member noted the existence of reservations about the extent to which the association should participate in social action, and a concern that NASW people might be seen as "crusaders." Some worried about the ability of busy chapters to engage in lobbying, but others countered that social action was one of the organization's major purposes (NASW, 1960a). Professional organizations such as NASW often struggle with the balance between professional development and broad social reform. At the same time that it promoted legislative activity, NASW established the Academy of Certified Social Workers as a credentialing mechanism and created a Committee on Private Practice (NASW, Board of Directors, 1961a).

The Council on Social Work Education had a narrower focus: the promotion of professional social work education. Yet it too felt it necessary to influence legislators and social welfare officials, particularly at the federal level. A good deal of CSWE's commitment to social action stemmed from the vision and experience of its first executive director, Ernest Witte. Witte assumed his position soon after CSWE was created by the merger of a graduate school association and an undergraduate education group in 1952. Witte had worked in several New Deal programs and served briefly as director of training in BPA. He was convinced of the importance of preparing qualified personnel for public agencies, and he brought good political connections to his work with the Council (Wolfe, 1992).

Where the NASW established formal mechanisms for social action, Witte tended toward an informal approach. He utilized not only on his own connections with legislators and government officials, but also called on deans of schools of social work and CSWE board members as needed to contact congressmen and government bureaucrats regarding legislative and policy issues. Witte's approach resembled that of social work educator Edith Abbott, a former mentor who established close ties with BPA as the bureau worked out its early training objectives. The council carried the interaction with government officials a step further by including a number of them on the CSWE board. Jane Hoey, for example, served as president of the board shortly after her retirement as director of BPA, and Wilbur Cohen, who spent much of his career in administrative posts in HEW, was a board member.

The CSWE records from the 1950s are full of letters from deans and board members to legislators and officials in support of social work training. The letter by Louisiana State University's Earl Klein to Senator Russell Long was one of many recommending support of the training provisions in the pending 1956 Social Security amendments. Klein assured Long that "the rehabilitative and restorative type of social service which is needed [in public welfare] requires graduate professional training" (Klein, 1956). Several years later, CSWE carried out another letter writing campaign urging support for training appropriations under the same amendments. These letters assured legislators that professional social work education for public assistance workers was basic for implementation of "individualization of service" in public assistance (Kidneigh, 1959). Such communications, while not always resulting in the requested action, did not go unnoticed. A staff member of the Senate Finance Committee, for example, expressed surprise at the large number of communications from schools of social work and asked who had organized such an extensive campaign (Witte, 1956).

The council worked with other social welfare organizations in promoting social work education and the professionalization of public assistance agencies. For example, both CSWE and NASW belonged to the National Social Welfare Assembly (NSWA), a loose federation of organizations interested in influencing social policy in the health and welfare arenas. CSWE and NASW were part of large group of representatives of voluntary social welfare groups that met with Arthur Flemming, secretary of HEW, in 1958. Following the meeting, Flemming pledged to support efforts to secure federal funds for research, training, and adequate coverage of services in public welfare (Summary Report, 1959). In these advocacy efforts, and in its relation to NASW, the council confined itself to its particular area of interest—the training and utilization of professional social workers. While the position was sometimes criticized for ignoring broader issues, it was one to which the council almost always adhered.

By the end of the 1950s, the two major social work organizations had developed a commitment to influencing public policy in the social welfare arena, and particularly in the field of public welfare. The 1956 amendments had signaled a move to a social services strategy that called for the use of professional social workers in public assistance agencies. Both organizations had gone on record in favor of such a strategy. The country was now about to enter a time of much turmoil regarding public welfare, a period that would involve NASW, CSWE, BPA, and social welfare organizations like APWA and NSWA in a concerted effort to change the program's approach.

On the eve of John F. Kennedy's election to the presidency, the United States was in the midst of its second recession in three years. Unemployment had gone up sharply. During the 1950s the welfare rolls had increased dramatically, in part due to a general liberalization of benefits. On average, ADC families spent more time on welfare than in 1950, and illegitimacy rates continued to rise. Finally, two events contributed to a rising sense of crisis in public welfare: the decision of the state of Louisiana to cut thousands of illegitimate children off the ADC roles, and a revolt against the welfare system in Newburgh, New York.

State rules that used illegitimate births as a factor in eligibility for ADC were not new in 1960. Many states had already attempted to remove illegitimate children and their families from the rolls (in cases, for example, where an out-of-wedlock pregnancy occurred after the mother had begun receiving welfare). These efforts at restriction were generally based on a "suitable home" policy—that is, the expectation that parents on ADC would maintain a home that met standards of health and care, and often, of morality. In 1935, Congress had agreed that the "moral character" of parents or caretakers could be considered in determining a child's eligibility for ADC. Due in part to resistance by BPA, however, only three states, all in the South, managed in the 1950s to legitimize laws or policies that used out-of-wedlock births as a factor in denying assistance (Coll, 1995).

In 1960, the state of Louisiana stunned the social welfare community by developing a restriction based on illegitimacy that within a period of several months cut twenty-three thousand children off the welfare rolls. Families received no advanced notice that they were losing their benefits, and were told that to requalify for aid they would have to submit proof that their "unsuitable home conditions" had been remedied. The process of reviewing cases promised to be a long one, involving lay parish welfare boards with limited time to spend. The story received broad coverage in the press. Local and national responses came swiftly (*Social Service Review*, 1960).

The Family Service Society of New Orleans joined the Urban League in petitioning city officials to provide emergency assistance for disqualified children. It also joined the numerous national organizations calling for an investigation by HEW to determine the conformity of the state plan to federal regulations. Many of these groups, including NASW, the Child Welfare League, CSWE, and the Family Service Association of America, filed friend of the court briefs at a subsequent hearing held by the commissioner of Social Security. The commissioner regretfully concluded that the lack of a federal requirement specifically prohibiting states from using "suitable home" as a factor in eligibility left him with no choice but to allow Louisiana to continue its policy. Yet in line with the suggestions of the social work and social welfare policy community, the secretary of HEW quickly ruled that no state could deprive a child of public assistance on grounds of an unsuitable home while the child still lived in that home. Assistance was to be continued while efforts were made to improve the home conditions or to arrange for the child's care elsewhere. The ruling thus built on a traditional child welfare principle that children in unfit homes were entitled to the protective services of the state (Family Services Association of America, 1961; Social Security Commission, 1961; Bell, 1965).

The next crisis in public welfare occurred about a year later, when Joseph Mitchell, the new city manager of Newburgh, New York, announced a thirteen-point plan to drastically curtail the city's ADC and general assistance programs. The move came in response to what citizens and most city officials saw as a "relief crisis," with welfare payments representing one-sixth of the city budget. Part of the increase in the rolls resulted from the fact that poor African-American migrant laborers, recruited to the area each summer to pick fruit, had begun to stay on as permanent residents. In addition, the city was undergoing an industrial decline and losing more affluent residents to the suburbs. Casting public welfare as the villain in the piece, the city manager's solution lay in a thirteen-point code that included such measures as limiting aid to most recipients to three months in a given year, denying benefits to mothers of illegitimate children who had additional children out of wedlock, and requiring all recipients other than those with disabilities to report monthly to the welfare department for a review of their cases.

While the "Newburgh Plan" received favorable response from cities and towns across the country, the professional welfare community was aghast (NASW, 1961; Grutzner, 1961). NASW and CSWE prepared a joint press release, citing Mitchell's thinking as leaning toward "the kind of 'ruthless dictatorship' which is completely at odds with American ideals and the democratic form of government." The release affirmed the importance of helping people to become as self-supporting as possible, but stressed society's responsibility to care for those who could not do so. However, the bulk of the organizations' criticism focused on Mitchell's disdain of social workers in the city's welfare department and his proposal to bring in untrained workers. The joint statement noted that such workers lacked "the years of training and experience necessary to provide effective family counseling which would enable many relief families to work out their personal difficulties and return to the ranks of the independent and self-supporting." Noting that skilled counseling by professional social workers, instead of money alone, was the best approach to reducing welfare costs, CSWE and NASW linked help to clients with the expansion of social work. The document ties the reduction of poverty to the intervention of professional social workers, thus imparting a self-serving quality to its message (NASW & CSWE, 1961).

The Newburgh code was subsequently struck down by a state court, but its challenge, along with the Louisiana incident, had served to galvanize social work and social welfare organizations and to solidify support for a different way to reduce the assistance rolls—the widespread provision of social services to those on welfare.

As we have seen, the importance of social services to improve family functioning and to increase independence had already been backed by various groups and by federal welfare officials in the 1950s. An increase in the number of trained social workers who could deliver such services was often added as a necessary corollary. The approach now seemed more important than ever, especially as a counterpoint to the growing revolt against public welfare and the increasing popularity of the belief that getting tough with clients would solve "welfare dependency." The time appeared right for the advancement of services: the two social work professional organizations had established a social action agenda and process; strong social welfare groups were ready to sell the services approach; and there were important insiders in the federal welfare bureaucracy as well as elected officials—notably the incoming president—who were sympathetic to the idea of positive and constructive welfare reform. These many individuals and groups worked hard and interacted in complex ways. Studies were made; reports spewed forth; and policy committee memberships overlapped. While a variety of recommendations for dealing with poverty emerged, the prevailing theme was the provision of services to welfare clients.

The first presidential committee devoted exclusively to public welfare was the Advisory Council on Public Assistance created by the Social Security Amendments of 1958. Members included Loula Dunn, an influential state public welfare administrator and director of APWA, and Wilbur Cohen. Cohen had a long history in federal social welfare programs, first as a staff person on the committee that created the Social Security Act and then as the assistant to the chair of the Social Security Board. By the 1950s he was an expert in both the technical and political aspects of federal health, welfare, and social security programs. Cohen left Washington in 1956 for a short stint on the faculty of the University of Michigan School of Social Work. Not a social worker himself, he nevertheless had much to contribute in the field of social policy. He in turn was influenced by the social work faculty with whom he worked, and especially by their focus on the psychological and social nature of people's problems. His experience at Michigan led him to a new stress on the blending of social services and income maintenance. Along with his friend and fellow social policy expert Elizabeth Wickenden, Cohen was to serve on a number of public welfare advisory bodies during the 1960s (Berkowitz, 1995).

Although the Council on Public Assistance began during the Eisenhower administration, its findings were utilized by Eisenhower's successor, John F. Kennedy. One of the group's recommendations was federal funding for general assistance (that is, welfare payments to all needy Americans, not just those in special categories), an idea that social work organizations had pushed ever since the Great Depression. The council also endorsed the 1956 Social Security Amendments and supported federally financed training for social workers to staff public welfare agencies. In addition to reviewing these recommendations, Kennedy looked to the suggestions of a Task Force on Health and Social Security that was developed at his request and chaired by Wilbur Cohen. Elizabeth Wickenden served as one of its members. Charged with developing health and welfare priorities for the new administration, this group's suggestions for improving public welfare included the strengthening of social services to needy families, children, and older persons; and the provision of federal funds for general assistance.

One step that had not been suggested in the Eisenhower council report was the recommendation that HEW be reorganized to bring about a linking of financial assistance, social services to ADC families, and those child welfare services traditionally overseen by the Children's Bureau (Task Force on Health and Social Security, 1961; Coll, 1995). Founded in 1912, the Children's Bureau had followed both a public health/preventive model in child welfare as well as a casework services approach. The bureau believed in pulling together all health and welfare activities related to children and did not limit its mission to poor children. BPA had a broader family focus and a specific charge of providing financial assistance to the poor. The bureau's social service capacities were less fully developed than those of the children's program. Thus although both BPA and the Children's Bureau were staffed by social workers, philosophical differences and turf battles often prevented them from working closely together. To Wickenden and others, this situation seemed an obstacle to reform.

Ideas about changes in public welfare came also from a source more closely connected to social work: the Project on Public Services for Families and Children, sponsored by the New York School of Social Work of Columbia University (now the Columbia University School of Social Work). Elizabeth Wickenden, who directed the project, traces its beginnings to informal discussions about public welfare problems among Justine Wise Polier, an influential domestic court judge; Fred DelliQuadri, the dean of the New York School; herself; and others interested in public assistance. Like Cohen, Wickenden was not a social worker, but she had developed close ties with the profession through positions in the New Deal's Federal Emergency Relief Administration and APWA, and consultant jobs with the Social Welfare Assembly and NASW (Wickenden, 1986–1987).

The discussions Wickenden describes led to the idea of an extensive study that would focus attention on governmental services for families and children. The New York School agreed to sponsor the project and the group secured funding from the Field Foundation. Social worker Winifred Bell (a Ph.D. student at the school) came on as Wickenden's assistant. The project's advisory committee included the executive directors of NASW, the Child Welfare League, and the Family Social Service Association of American; Jane Hoey; and people with experience in running state public welfare departments. Cohen and several New York School faculty served as consultants.

The major thrust of the study was an organizational analysis of the effects of maintaining separate programs for child welfare and public assistance within HEW. The project's underlying goal was the integration and strengthening of "governmental resources for child welfare . . . , assistance to needy families, and community welfare services in a coordinated program of family and children's services" (Wickenden & Bell, 1961). While project participants acknowledged the role of societal malfunctioning in the creation of poverty, their stress was clearly on amelioration, or the ways in which a service-based public welfare system could help the "individual victim of social disorder" (Wickenden & Bell, 1961, p. 20). Basically, the importance of services was a given, and the project's major question was how best to organize the service initiative at the federal level.

To shed light on issues related to the organization and goals of social services, the project sent a ten-question "letter of inquiry" to about 350 leaders in the field. These included all state public welfare commissioners, the directors of all national voluntary organizations involved in child and family welfare, and the deans of all the schools of social work. Out of their responses, project staff and advisors distilled these and other proposals, published in a final report in 1961: (1) the federal public assistance and child welfare programs should be combined in a new Family and Child Welfare Program within HEW; (2) the new program should provide federal grants to the states for public welfare services aimed at promoting child and family welfare; and (3) the program should make available grants for the training of social workers and other welfare personnel, and for research and demonstration projects in the field of child and family welfare (Wickenden & Bell, 1961). The final report was published and pre-publication page proofs sent to Abraham Ribicoff, Kennedy's newly appointed secretary of HEW.

In the early 1960s, then, a formal study and two advisory committees had put forth their ideas for an improved welfare system. Social workers had directly or indirectly influenced many of these recommendations. At the same time, social work professional organizations were developing their own position statements and seeking ways to promote them to policymakers. Many of these stances coincided with those of others interested in expanding social welfare measures, but included a particular stress on professional issues of staffing and training in public welfare.

The National Association of Social Workers' legislative agenda for 1961 emerged out of a many-layered process in which objectives were developed by the Commission on Social Policy, submitted to representatives of a large number of chapters for discussion and review, laid before the board of directors, and after further discussion, approved by the board for presentation to all the chapters. Thus while the resulting platform no doubt included compromises, it was probably a reasonable representation of what many social workers (at least those who belonged to NASW) felt to be important recommendations for change. Those items "of continuing interest and concern" included appropriations and additional amendments to the Social Security Act. First on the list was an increase in the appropriation for social welfare research and the provision of funds for "training of personnel for services to families and children." Regarding amendments to the Social Security Act, the association stressed health care benefits for those covered by Social Security (one of Kennedy's priorities), as well as federal leadership and funding to support a coordinated federal program of public assistance and services to families, children, and the elderly. Thus NASW echoed the calls of other groups for reorganization within HEW and the development of services, but moved the recommendation of funding for training to the top of the agenda.

However, as a balance to the stress on an individualized service approach, the association also gave high priority to the protection of migratory workers, equality of opportunity for African-Americans, and the development of the Peace Corps. Secondary emphasis went to economic development of depressed areas and an increase in the minimum wage. The association's legislative objectives the following year added an increase in public assistance payments, the extension of family-centered services to all persons in need (not just those on ADC), higher benefits and training programs for the unemployed, and a public employment program that included public works (NASW, 1960b; no date).

The association presented several of its planks to the Democratic and Republican parties. Its HEW Liaison Committee conferred with federal officials, including the commissioner of Social Security and the heads of HEW operating agencies. Rudolph Danstedt, director of the association's Washington office, appeared frequently before congressional committees to present NASW's point of view. He earned high praise for his effectiveness from Representative John Fogarty, a highly influential figure in the determination of appropriations for HEW (NASW, Board of Directors, 1962). The association also encouraged state and local chapters to support the NASW agenda by promoting it to their congressmen and senators.

The Council on Social Work Education also stepped up its lobbying activities as the new presidential administration began its work. CSWE and NASW established a division of labor in which the council focused concern on educational matters but also had official representation on the NASW Commission on Social Policy and the HEW Liaison Committee. The CSWE board voted to renew action to promote federal funds for training social workers in public welfare, in close coordination with the NASW Washington office, NSWA, and other national organizations. Witte continued his lobbying of federal officials and used his dean's network to make contacts with legislators. Witte wrote, for example, to William Mitchell, who had replaced Schottland as commissioner of Social Security. The CSWE director urged Mitchell to give highest priority to grants for schools of social work in his legislative recommendations to the new administration. Training funds were particularly crucial for public assistance work, a field "grossly discriminated against . . . and where the need for qualified personnel is especially acute." Mitchell reported back that his office had already begun to prepare the ground for the administration's approval of training grants and that Secretary Ribicoff seemed sympathetic to the idea (Witte, 1960; Mitchell, 1960).

In its promotion of social work education, CSWE was supported by a new organization, the National Citizens Committee on Careers in Social Work. Sponsored jointly by CSWE and NASW, the committee sought not only to explain and promote social work education to the public, but to lobby actively for federal funding of that education and to mobilize citizen support in this endeavor. Elizabeth Wickenden consulted with the Citizens Committee on legislative strategies. She also warned them about the negative attitude toward social workers she encountered among congressmen, noting that "the principal obstacle to support for training social workers is the lack of enthusiasm for social work programs, particularly public welfare." On the other hand, officials like Wilbur Cohen, returning to Washington as assistant secretary of HEW, could be counted on for support (National Citizens Committee on Careers in Social Work, 1961). In response to a letter from Witte congratulating him on his new position, Cohen wrote that he would "work my darndest to earn the confidence and trust you've placed in me" (Cohen, 1961).

The stage was set, networks developed, sympathetic government officials identified. The curtain was about to rise on social work's major part in the establishment of a federal social services initiative in public welfare—consultation with HEW secretary Ribicoff. Ribicoff's most recent experience before his cabinet post in the Kennedy administration was as governor of Connecticut, a state with high welfare costs. One of his earliest decisions as secretary was to take a thorough look at the existing welfare system (Coll, 1995). Cohen, as assistant secretary, encouraged him in this endeavor. According to Cohen's biographer, Edward Berkowitz (1995), the assistant secretary "started on welfare reform the day he arrived in Washington" (p. 146). While Ribicoff had before him the reports of Eisenhower's advisory council and Kennedy's Social Security task force, which Cohen had chaired, he wanted further information from social work leaders and the broader welfare professional community. He turned first to NASW, and met with members of the association's HEW Liaison Committee in February 1961. Reporting on that meeting later, one committee member described their growing realization that this was not going to follow the pattern of earlier, more informational sessions with HEW secretaries. Instead, the group soon saw that Ribicoff was looking to them for advice— for "guidance and help with respect to the nature of [federal] welfare programs . . . and the future direction of such programs." Ribicoff said he intended to review the welfare program and to recommend changes to Congress in 1962, and he invited NASW to contribute to this process (NASW, Board of Directors, 1961a).

Duly impressed, the liaison committee drafted a memo proposing that consideration be given to the ways in which welfare services could help prevent family disorganization and dependency. Upon reviewing the

memo, Ribicoff asked Cohen and the committee to set up a meeting of representatives of key welfare groups. This became the Ad Hoc Committee on
Public Welfare, with a large number of representatives of NASW, including the chair. Other groups involved included APWA, CSWE, NSWA, the
Child Welfare League, and the Family Services Association (NASW, Board
of Directors, 1961a). The committee presented its report with recommendations for welfare reform at a three-hour meeting with Ribicoff. Similar
to all the other reports, but with even greater emphasis, the Ad Hoc Committee's document called for the development of "accelerated and intensified rehabilitative services aimed at reducing family breakdown and
chronic dependency," and a ten-year target date for appropriate training
of public welfare personnel, with the goal that one-third of all social workers in public welfare would have an MSW. The committee also endorsed a
single category of relief for all poor families (not just single-parent ones) as
well as research and development projects, including a comprehensive
national study of the causes of illegitimacy (NASW, Board of Directors,
1961b; Ad Hoc Committee on Public Welfare, 1961, pp. 3, 5).

Ribicoff reacted positively to the committee's recommendations, and in
subsequent speeches indicated that he was considering legislation that
reflected many of the group's priorities. But the chief architect of the 1962
Social Security amendments was Wilbur Cohen (Berkowitz, 1995). The
proposed legislation embraced the idea of rehabilitative services, requiring states to provide such services and establishing a 75 percent federal
match for their costs. The bill also gave federal support to unemployment
measures, such as community work and training programs. To increase
the skills of public welfare staff, the bill authorized Congress to provide
funds for grants to colleges and universities to train personnel and for fel-
lowships to individuals pursuing such training. While the legislation did
not define "services" clearly, professional staff in BPA understood these to
mean casework by trained social workers and traditional services such as
homemakers and foster care (Derthick, 1975). Reflecting the interest of
Cohen and welfare analysts such as Wickenden in reorganizing the welfare program, the bill called for coordination between child welfare personnel and public welfare staff in providing child welfare services.

NASW, CSWE and other social work and social welfare groups lobbied
vigorously for the proposed amendments. Representatives of these groups
testified in favor of the bill before the House Ways and Means Committee.
The president of NASW spoke in support of the Kennedy administration's
vision of a "'rehabilitative road' to the alleviation and prevention of economic and social poverty" (U.S. House of Representatives, 1962, p. 428).
The chair of the NASW/CSWE Committee on Careers in Social Work testified regarding the need for trained social work personnel. He cited evidence from public welfare demonstration programs that counseling by

trained social workers reduced the welfare rolls. Elizabeth Wickenden presented the findings of the public services project; representatives of APWA, NSWA, the Child Welfare League, and the National Conference of Catholic Charities also appeared.

The fact that the bill appealed to both conservatives and liberals in its promise to restore independence helped it move quickly through Congress. When Kennedy signed the bill into law in July 1962, he reiterated its objectives of preventing or reducing welfare dependency. The expectation—developed by Ribicoff, Cohen, and many social work and social welfare professionals—that the welfare rolls would soon diminish, was to spell trouble for the services approach in the months and years ahead.

After the legislation's passage, NASW encouraged chapters to promote the necessary legislative changes at the state level, emphasizing services and professional training. A CSWE Deans' Advisory Committee to HEW, set up at Cohen's request, advised federal officials on educational standards and policies for the Children's Bureau and the Bureau of Public Assistance (now called the Bureau of Family Services, or BFS), for use when training funds became available. But it quickly became apparent that the 1962 amendments would not immediately usher in a golden age of welfare reform. The NASW Commission on Social Policy had already recognized that the amendments did not possess "a charmed panacea" for correcting the problems of dependency, which stemmed from such factors as discrimination, lack of health care, and inadequate education, as well as family breakdown (NASW, 1963). And both organizations were concerned when Congress failed to authorize the amendments' training appropriations in 1962 and 1963.

Administration of the new act by HEW was also problematic. Assistant Secretary Cohen, following the act's call for coordination of child welfare and public welfare personnel and due to his own predilection for an integrated child and family services program, suggested removing BFS from the Social Security Administration and placing both it and the Children's Bureau under a new Welfare Administration within HEW. In late 1962, Anthony Celebreeze, who had replaced Ribicoff as secretary, approved both the new structure and the appointment of Ellen Winston as its head. Cohen and others had great hopes for Winston, an experienced and active public welfare administrator who had been involved in both APWA and CSWE. But Winston had administrative difficulties. Some related to her own problems with delegating tasks and working smoothly with state administrators, but others to the sheer challenge of applying a vaguely defined services approach and improving the public welfare staffing situation. In addition, long-lasting differences in philosophy between the Children's Bureau and BFS meant that the two units remained as divided as ever (Berkowitz, 1995; Coll, 1995).

The services approach of the 1962 amendments was predicated on the increased skills and professionalism of state and local public welfare personnel. Yet lack of congressional appropriations for training hindered staff improvement. In addition, the social work education community failed to develop a realistic plan for providing a competent public welfare work force. More specifically, the graduate social work education community, which dominated CSWE, had great difficulty in overcoming its ambivalence about the value of undergraduate social work education for entry-level social work practice. This reflected long-standing tensions between graduate and undergraduate educators, which had been only partially resolved by the merger of the two groups in CSWE (Leighninger, 1987).

Ernest Witte expressed concern about the council's position soon after the amendments had passed. He felt uneasy, he reported to the CSWE board, that CSWE didn't appear to be dealing with basic manpower issues. A board member agreed, noting that although about 75 percent of all social work positions were filled by people without a graduate degree, the council continued to maintain that undergraduate social work education prepared people only for graduate education, and not for practice (CSWE, Board of Directors, 1962). Board discussions over the next few years indicated great ambivalence over relinquishing the position that graduate education constituted the only path to professionalism, despite the growth of undergraduate programs and the realization that schools of social work could never provide sufficient MSW practitioners to staff the public welfare system. This inability to train enough welfare staff was a bone of contention, for example, among welfare administrators in New York City, who complained to Winston about the reluctance of the deans of the city's schools of social work to take steps to accommodate the large number of employees eligible for educational leave (CSWE, Board of Directors, 1964). Yet while recognizing the problem, CSWE leadership was often skeptical about finding ways to resolve it without compromising "standards" in social work education. Many argued that CSWE's primary responsibility was to promote quality in graduate social work education, and that undergraduate social work education should consist only of a good liberal arts background with some courses on the field of social welfare. While CSWE could perhaps offer help to undergraduate social welfare curricula and agency in-service training programs, the council should be conscious of its limitations in preparing staff (CSWE, Board of Directors, 1964).

Others in the council objected to this stance. Katherine Kendall, who had succeeded Witte as executive director, posed a number of questions regarding the organization's role in modifying graduate education and helping to develop undergraduate education as preparation for practice. Board discussion of these issues included the argument that CSWE should be doing more to meet the needs of public agencies for competent personnel at the baccalaureate level. The beginnings of a consensus were sketched in a board-approved statement that CSWE recognized an obligation to extend its concerns beyond its "continuing core responsibility for . . . professional [i.e., graduate] education to the broader scope of training and education to meet all social work manpower needs" (CSWE, Board of Directors, 1965).

These needs were much on the mind of welfare bureaucrats within HEW. Cohen, in fact, had written Kendall of his intention to help social work education secure funds for new and expanded schools of social work (Cohen, 1965). Yet HEW's interest extended to undergraduate social work education as well. In 1963, at the advice of a social worker and training expert in BFS, Cohen set up a U.S. Task Force on Social Work Education and Manpower to make recommendations on overcoming the shortage of trained social workers. A committee of social work deans served as an advisory group. The task force report, *Closing the Gap in Social Work Manpower* (1965), projected a need for one hundred thousand new professional social workers for public programs by 1970. To meet this need, the group called for expanded facilities and student aid for graduate training, but also emphasized the importance of advancement of undergraduate social work education for direct entry into practice (Austin, Antonyappan, & Leighninger, 1996).

Social work organizations, and particularly CSWE, were delighted when President Johnson highlighted the importance of social workers in his "Domestic Health and Education Message" to Congress in March 1966. Referring to the manpower study, he noted the many "unfilled vacancies for qualified social workers, at a time when we need their skills more than ever before," and said he had asked the secretary of HEW, now John Gardner, to consult with social work educational leaders to develop recommendations for overcoming the shortage (Pins, 1966). Ironically, recognition of the importance of social work training was on the ascendance at the same time that social work's orientation and methods were being called into question by those involved in planning and implementing President Johnson's War on Poverty. Social work relationships with the new poverty programs were much different from their relationships with HEW and its units. A number of professional social workers were administrators or staff members of the various bureaus and offices in HEW; important figures like Cohen were sympathetic to social work issues and concerns during much of the 1960s. In contrast, the War on Poverty agenda emerged from outside HEW. Its key players were social scientists, and particularly economists, rather than welfare officials. The poverty program was directed by the White House, not HEW, and people like Cohen were only peripherally involved (Critchlow & Hawley, 1989; Berkowitz, 1995).

Social workers like Richard Cloward played crucial roles in Mobilization for Youth, an important precursor to the War on Poverty, and others helped staff programs like Head Start and VISTA. But by and large, social workers and their professional organizations had mixed feelings about the poverty programs. Witte and other CSWE board members were skeptical about Kennedy's Peace Corp proposal, which, while not a part of the later U.S. antipoverty initiative, had a similar stress on community self-help and interventions by nonprofessionals. It was headed by Sargent Shriver, who would later take charge of the Office of Economic Opportunity (OEO). While CSWE wondered whether "younger inexpert persons sent abroad could serve a purpose," the council decided that since the program was politically popular, they should write to Shriver offering assistance (Witte, 1961). The council's reaction to the Head Start program was much more enthusiastic, probably in part because the group was asked directly for input by its director, Julius Richmond. Kendall assured Richmond of CSWE's wholehearted support for this comprehensive approach to the welfare of children, and noted that they were working to expand social work education at both the graduate and undergraduate levels to meet the staffing needs of this and other poverty initiatives (Kendall, 1965a).

Perhaps most problematic for social work was its tenuous relationship with OEO. Although NASW and CSWE publicly supported many of the War on Poverty programs and lobbied for passage of the Economic Opportunity Act, they were not included in the inner circle of planners and administrators of the antipoverty initiative. In an attempt have an impact on planning and implementation, representatives of NASW requested a meeting with Shriver, then the president's special assistant on the War on Poverty, in May 1964. Since Shriver was involved with the pending Economic Opportunity Act legislation, they met instead with another planning official and members of his staff. The NASW representatives first reaffirmed their support of the pending legislation, then commented at length about the extensive employment of "less than fully trained personnel"—i.e., nonprofessionals—in the programs under the act. The group acknowledged the need for less than trained professionals, and stressed the contribution that social workers could make toward training such personnel. Reading between the lines, one senses that while NASW knew it could not prevent the use of nonprofessionals, it sought to assert some control through being given responsibility for staff training. The representatives outlined additional ways in which the association could make contributions to the development of the OEO program. The planning official's response was to suggest an NASW advisory committee to consult with the poverty staff (NASW, OEO Subcommittee, 1964).

However, an active consultation role for social workers never really materialized. In subsequent meetings of the advisory committee with

Shriver and OEO staff, committee representatives expressed concern about what seemed "a critical attitude on the part of 'key' OEO personnel" toward welfare programs and possibly toward social work (NASW, OEO Subcommittee, 1964). It appeared that in the upper echelons of OEO, social work was equated with "the traditional way" of doing things. The committee raised issues regarding the use of untrained personnel in social work jobs, the ability of the poor to become significantly involved in programs designed to help them, and the tendency of OEO to equate those programs that were not "opportunity geared" as "handouts" (NASW, OEO Subcommittee, 1965). All in all, despite social work's assurances of support for the OEO programs, and some outreach attempts by OEO administrators and staff, it was clear that social workers and War on Poverty leaders differed on basic philosophies (e.g., "offering opportunities" vs. "providing rehabilitative services" to the poor) and on ways of staffing antipoverty programs (NASW, OEO Subcommittee, 1965). Despite the meetings, social work's influence over the poverty program did not increase. Symbolically, after asking NASW for names of candidates for a National Advisory Council on OEO, Shriver failed to appoint a single social worker to the council.

In some ways, social work's lack of influence within the War on Poverty stemmed from the profession's inability to abandon traditional, casework-oriented approaches and an obsession with professional staffing of welfare and poverty programs where at all possible. Within the OEO context, social work appeared to be an outdated field concerned with services rather than with increasing poor people's control over their own lives. It is significant that while social workers lobbied for the poverty programs, they also maintained that there would always be people who needed individualized treatment. Perhaps this is evidence that social work abandoned the poor. Yet in some ways, social work organizations moved *beyond* the War on Poverty in the mid- to late 1960s, by adding the guarantee of an adequate standard of living as a right of all Americans to their policy agenda. By 1964, for example, NASW had adopted the principle that whether it be through a system of family allowances or a negative income tax program, income maintenance should be joined with the social insurances, public welfare, and the poverty programs to ensure that every American would have his or her minimum economic needs met (NASW, 1966). The association was the first national professional organization to take such a stand.

Although NASW, CSWE, and other social welfare organizations looked to the continued strengthening of the public welfare component of meeting people's needs, the goals of public welfare were rapidly changing. By the end of the decade, the focus on social services, never fully implemented and its effectiveness now being questioned by research (see, e.g.,

Meyer & Borgatta, 1965), had begun to give way to an emphasis on work. Soon Congress, under the leadership of House Ways and Means Committee Chair Wilbur Mills, would begin the steady move toward work incentives and requirements that has become a familiar feature of AFDC.

Evidence that the tide was turning came with HEW secretary Gardner's response to the recommendations of the last major study of public welfare in the 1960s, the Advisory Council on Public Welfare's *"Having the Power, We Have the Duty"* (1966). The council was created by the 1962 amendments to review the public assistance and child welfare programs and to make suggestions for improvement. It worked closely with Ellen Winston, head of the Welfare Administration. The group was chaired by Fedele Fauri, the dean of the University of Michigan School of Social Work, and included social work administrators who had been active in NASW, state public welfare administrators, the head of the Urban League, and the consummate public welfare consultant, Elizabeth Wickenden.

The council reported to Gardner in 1966. Its recommendations took the services approach and the provision of financial assistance one final step, by proposing that adequate financial aid and social services be made available to all who needed them "as a matter of right." Services should be provided by public agencies to people of all incomes. The federal government should set nationwide standards for services and a required minimum income, and assume financial responsibility for costs over a stipulated state share. The existing state and federal roles would thus be reversed, with the federal government establishing standards and determining the amount to be spent. The report also recommended that existing work training programs be made a permanent part of the public welfare structure. Finally, it called for greater support of education and training for personnel at all levels, yet recognized social work as the "core profession" in public welfare.

Gardner, however, paid little attention to the report. There was no press release announcing its recommendations; its only publicity was a short summary in an HEW journal six months later. Gardner had his own ideas about welfare changes, ideas that did not coincide with those of the social work and social welfare experts on the Advisory Council. Much disappointed by this outcome, and probably also by the lack of success of the Welfare Administration in implementing the services approach, Winston resigned her post (Coll, 1995; Wickenden, 1986–1987).

Gardner now felt free to bring about a major reorganization of the welfare programs within HEW. This change was based on a belief in the ability of rehabilitation, and particularly vocational rehabilitation, to change dependent people into independent ones (Berkowitz, 1991). Based on this conviction, in 1967 Gardner created a new agency, the Social and Rehabilitation Service (SRS), to be headed by Mary Switzer, the long-time director of the vocational rehabilitation program within HEW. Gardner moved the Bureau of Family Services and the Children's Bureau into SRS, along with several other welfare programs. While the new agency would emphasize services, these would now be specifically directed at getting people into employment.

With Winston's resignation and the embrace of a vocational rehabilitation approach, the social workers in BFS saw the handwriting on the wall. Their dominance in public welfare would now be greatly curtailed. It did not help that Switzer didn't particularly like social workers (Wolfe, 1992). Whole divisions and units of the vocational rehabilitation program were transferred into SRS. If these entities overlapped those of BFS or the Children's Bureau, such as personnel departments, the units were merged, and an SRS person put in charge. Most importantly, SRS changed the way in which services would be provided by state public welfare programs. As Coll (1995) notes, the basis for social services had been the idea of counseling by the family caseworker, who also did the initial assessment of client eligibility for the program. The SRS administration "killed this concept promptly . . . by separating eligibility determination from all other social services" (p. 246).

New welfare legislation made further changes in public welfare. The public welfare portion of the 1967 Social Security amendments included a major counterpart to the social services approach—a new workfare program. The legislative process took place in the context of rising welfare rolls and costs, devastating "race riots," or civil disturbances, in Newark and Detroit, and an increasingly militant welfare rights movement. These led the House Ways and Means Committee toward repressive, rather than liberalizing approaches to public welfare. The initial House bill would have mandated the referral of many women on AFDC directly to employment or to work training programs. The final act, however, was toned down and more comprehensive, in part due to fears that a tougher welfare program would have resulted in further rioting. The major focus of the legislation was the requirement that all women be referred to work or to a training program *unless* to do so would affect the well-being of the family, or the mother was unable to work due to illness. In practice, this excused a fair number of women. To implement this goal, the law established the Work Incentive Program (WIN), which was administered by the U.S. Department of Labor. Under WIN, child care was to be provided when needed by working mothers. In addition, employed AFDC recipients would be allowed to keep a portion of the incomes they earned, rather than having the whole amount subtracted from their assistance checks. Yet even in this softer version, the WIN program established a new direction for AFDC—the expectation that mothers on welfare should enter the workforce.

Social work organizations do not appear to have led much of an opposition to the work requirements of the 1967 amendments. The CSWE board specifically decided not to "concern itself" with the public welfare sections of the legislation (CSWE, Board of Directors, 1967). The social work community was instead dazzled by the potential of the amendments to finally provide significant funding to social work education. With help from social workers within BFS, the continued support of Wilbur Cohen, and the profession's own intense lobbying effort, Section 707 of the Social Security Amendments provided $5 million a year for three years for federal grants to both undergraduate departments and graduate schools of social work. The funding would help cover the costs of developing, expanding, or improving social work educational programs. With the exception of the first year, when only $3 million was actually appropriated, the full amount was provided (Austin, Antonyappan, & Leighninger, 1996).

Social work could boast a major victory in 1967—yet for proponents of the profession's role in public welfare, the victory was a hollow one. The idea of federally supported social work training had been closely tied to the vision of social workers as the skilled providers of services in a reformed public welfare system. Yet by the end of the 1960s, a belief in social services as the best way to improve welfare had lost ground. In addition, the major federal agency promoting social work as the core public welfare profession was losing its influence and its control over services spending (Derthick, 1975). Finally, despite the goals of the professional organizations and BFS, people who received social work graduate and undergraduate social work degrees in the 1960s did not necessarily flock to public welfare jobs. As Cohen once noted to Witte, the social work profession was not always eager to help the cause of welfare reform and did not encourage students to work in public assistance (Berkowitz, 1995).

Was social work's interest in expanding professional education simply self-serving? Was the emphasis on a services approach to welfare largely aimed at legitimizing the profession? By pursuing this approach over others, did social work abandon the poor? Yes and no. It is true that had it been more flexible, the social work educational community could have created a more practical program of training for public welfare staff. As Kendall (1965b) told her board in 1965, "[D]eep concern about the present manpower situation has led [me] to the conclusion that we have failed to solve the problem precisely because, as a professional group, we have never taken responsibility for it in a positive way." In addition, social work often seemed to be defending its turf in the public welfare system, as seen in its dismissal of the ability of others, particularly "untrained staff," to be helpful to clients. And, it could be argued, the services approach substituted counseling for what clients really needed—jobs that paid a living wage, an end to racial discrimination, and so forth.

On the other hand, social work educators gradually began to accept the idea of a multilevel staffing pattern that included undergraduate-level social work practitioners and others. The services stress was promoted by many groups, and was not simply an invention of the social work profession. It was also not the only recommendation made by social workers to deal with the problem of persistent poverty. Social work organizations promoted the social insurances; lobbied for War on Poverty initiatives; called for a single, adequately funded category of relief for all poor people; and then moved to a stress on income maintenance programs. Like many other groups and professions in the 1960s, social workers were caught up in a period of rapid social and economic change, and like others, they were not always able to adjust.

Key to Archival Sources

NA: National Archives, Washington, D.C.
SHSW: State Historical Society of Wisconsin, Madison, WI
SWHA: Social Welfare History Archives, University of Minnesota, Minneapolis, MN

REFERENCES

Ad Hoc Committee on Public Welfare (1961). *Recommendations for Public Welfare Reorganization.* Box 11, folder: Ad Hoc Committee on Public Welfare, 11/1/61, NASW Records, Washington Office, SWHA.

Advisory Council on Public Welfare (1966). *"Having the Power, We Have the Duty," Summary of the Recommendations to the Secretary of Health, Education, and Welfare.* Washington, DC: Welfare Administration, HEW.

Anderson, J. (1955). Memos, 1/14/55 and 4/21/55, to Members of TIAC Commission on Social Policy and Social Action. Folder 951, NASW: TIAC, Social Policy and Action Committee, ForNASW, 1955, NASW Records, SWHA.

Austin, M. J., Antonyappan, J. M., and Leighninger, L. (1966). Federal support for social work education: Section 707 of the 1967 Social Security Amendments. *Social Service Review, 70*(1), 83–97. Bell, W. (1965). *Aid to Dependent Children.* New York: Columbia University Press.

Berkowitz, E. D. (1991). *America's Welfare State: From Roosevelt to Reagan.* Baltimore: Johns Hopkins University Press.

Berkowitz, E. D. (1995). *Mr. Social Security: The Life of Wilbur J. Cohen.* Lawrence: University of Kansas Press.

Cohen, W. (1961). Letter to Ernest Witte, 3/15/61. Record Group XX, Box 24, folder: U.S. Health, Education, and Welfare, Dept. of, Commissioner Secretary Correspondence (Gen.), CSWE Records, SWHA.

Cohen, W. (1965). Letter to Katherine Kendall, 5/11/65. Record Group XX, Box 24, folder: U.S. Health, Education, and Welfare, Dept. of, Commissioner Secretary Correspondence (Gen.), CSWE Records, SWHA.

Coll, B. D. (1995). *Safety Net: Welfare and Social Security, 1929–1979*. New Brunswick, NJ: Rutgers University Press.

Critchlow, D. T., & Hawley, E. W. (1989). Introduction to Chapter 9. In *Poverty and Public Policy in Modern America*. Chicago, IL: Dorsey.

CSWE, Board of Directors (1962). Minutes, 5/27/62. Master Issuances, Box M- 16, folder: 62-16, CSWE Records, SWHA.

CSWE, Board of Directors (1965). Minutes, 11/28–30/65. Master Issuances, Box M26, folder: 66-16 (1-28), CSWE Records, SWHA.

CSWE, Board of Directors (1967). Minutes, 3/30–31/67. Master Issuances, Box M29, folder: 61-16, CSWE Records, SWHA.

CSWE (1964). Issues for policy determination, 10/16/64. Master Issuances, Box M15, folder: 64-16, CSWE Records, SWHA.

Derthick, M. (1975). *Uncontrollable Spending for Social Services Grants*. Washington, DC: Brookings Institution.

Ehrenreich, J. H. (1985). *The Altruistic Imagination: A History of Social Work and Social Policy in the United States*. Ithaca, NY: Cornell University Press.

Family Services Association of America (1961). Memo, 12/4/61. Record Group XXXI, Box 12, folder: Social Work, Social Policy and Action by CSWE, CSWE Records, SWHA.

Grutzner, G. (1961). Newburgh policy has wide support. *New York Times*, 24 June.

Kendall, K. (1965a). Letter to Julius Richmond, 2/17/65. Record Group XX, Box 24, folder: Office of Economic Opportunity, CSWE Records, SWHA.

Kendall, K. (1965b). Memo to Board of Directors, CSWE, 9/24/65. Master Issuances, Box M-22, folder: 65-16, CSWE Records, SWHA.

Kidneigh, J. C. (1959). Letter to Fred Marshall, House of Representatives, 3/17/59. Record Group XXXI, Box 12, folder: Social Work, Social Policy and Action by CSWE, CSWE Records, SWHA.

Klein, E. (1956). Letter to Hon. Russell Long, 3/5/56. Record Group XXXI, Box 12, folder: Social Work, Social Policy and Action by CSWE, CSWE Records, SWHA.

Leighninger, L. (1987). *Social Work: Search for Identity*. Westport, CT: Greenwood.

Meyer, H. J. and Borgatta, E. F. (1965). *Girls at Vocational High*. New York: Russell Sage.

Mitchell, W. I. (1960). Letter to Ernest Witte, 12/30/60. Record Group XXXI, Box 12, folder: Social Work, Social Policy and Action by CSWE, CSWE Records, SWHA.

NASW & CSWE (1961). Press Release. Record Group XXXI, Box 12, folder: Social Work, Social Policy and Action, CSWE Records, SWHA.

NASW (1959). Working paper on social action. Box 5, folder: Task Force on Social Action, 1959–1960, NASW Records, Washington Office, SWHA.

NASW (1960a). Meeting of Task Force #5—Social Action of NASW Structure Review Committee, April. Box 5, folder: Task Force on Social Action, 1959–1960, NASW Records, Washington Office, SWHA.

NASW (1960b). 1961 NASW Federal Legislative Objectives. Box 5, folder: Legislative Priorities, 1958–1961, NASW Records, Washington Office, SWHA.

NASW (1961). Will the Newburgh Plan work in your city? Fact sheet. New York: Author.

NASW (1963). Washington Memorandum, January. Box 5, Legislative Objectives, 1962–1963, NASW Records, Washington Office, SWHA.

NASW (1966). Income Maintenance, Statement by Commission on Social Policy, 7/22/66. Box 11, folder: Income Maintenance, NASW Records, Washington Office, SWHA.

NASW (no date). 1962 legislative objectives of the National Association of Social Workers for public welfare—for the unemployed—and statement on work relief (ca. 1961). Box 11, folder: Public Welfare, NASW Records, Washington Office, SWHA.

NASW, Board of Directors (1961a). Minutes, 5/12–13/61. NASW Records, Washington Office, SWHA.

NASW, Board of Directors (1961b). Minutes, 12/14–16/61. NASW Records, Washington Office, SWHA.

NASW, Board of Directors (1962). Minutes, 3/29–31/62. NASW Records, Washington Office, SWHA.

NASW, OEO Subcommittee (1964). OEO Subcommittee Meeting, 9/25/64. Box 7, NASW Records, Washington Office, SWHA.

NASW, OEO Subcommittee (1965). Subcommittee Meeting, OEO, 7/15–16/65. Box 7, NASW Records, Washington Office, SWHA.

National Citizens Committee on Careers in Social Work (1961). Minutes, 1/16/61. Record Group XXXI, Box 12, folder: Social Work, Social Policy and Action by CSWE, CSWE Records, SWHA.

Pins, A., Acting Executive Director, CSWE (1966). Memo to Board of Directors, 3/2/66. Master Issuances, Box M-26, folder: 66-16 (1-28), CSWE Records, SWHA.

Schottland, C. I. (1965). *Reminiscences*, Oral History, Social Security Project. New York: Columbia University, Oral History Research Office.

Social Security Commission (1961). Minutes, Meeting of the Social Security Commissioner and Welfare Commissioner. Box 29, Notebook: DHEW, Soc. Sec. Admin. Official Commissioner's Action Minutes, 1/58–1/63, Record Group 47, Social Security Administration Records, NA.

Social Service Review (1960). Hungry children in Louisiana. Notes and Comments. *Social Service Review, 34,* 4.

Specht, R., & Courtney, M. E. (1994). *Unfaithful Angels: How Social Work Has Abandoned Its Mission.* New York: Free Press.

Summary Report (1959). Summary report, meeting of the Sec. of HEW with representatives of national voluntary organizations concerned with Social Security, 11/19/58. Record Group XX, Organizations and Agencies, Box 23, CSWE Records, SWHA.

Task Force on Health and Social Security (1961). Health and security for the American people. A Report to President-Elect John F. Kennedy, January 10, 1961. Box 1, folder: Kennedy Task Force, 1960–1961, Elizabeth Wickenden Papers, SHSW.

U.S. House of Representatives (1962). *Public Welfare Amendments of 1962, Hearings before the Committee on Ways and Means,* 87th Congress, 2nd Session, on HR 10023—A Bill to Extend and Improve the Public Assistance and Child Welfare Services Programs of the Social Security Act, February 7, 9, and 13, 1962. Washington, DC: United States Government Printing Office.

U.S. Task Force on Social Work Education and Manpower (1965). *Closing the Gap in Social Work Manpower*. Washington, DC: U.S. Department of Health, Education, and Welfare.

Wenocur, S., & Reisch, M. (1989). *From Charity to Enterprise: The Development of American Social Work in a Market Economy*. Chicago: University of Illinois Press.

Wickenden, E. (1986–1987). *Oral History by Jean Bandler*. MS 800, Box 16, Folder 3, Elizabeth Wickenden Papers, SHSW.

Wickenden, E., & Bell, W. (1961). *Public Welfare: Time for a Change*. Report of the Project on Public Services for Families and Children. New York: New York School of Social Work of Columbia University.

Witte, E. (1956). Letter to Sidney Hollander, 4/16/56. Record Group XXXI, Box 12, folder: Social Work, Social Policy and Action by CSWE, CSWE Records, SWHA.

Witte, E. (1960). Letter to William L. Mitchell, 12/23/60. Record Group XXXI, Box 12, folder: Social Work, Social Policy and Action by CSWE, CSWE Records, SWHA.

Witte, E. (1961). Memo for file, 4/6/61. Record Group XX, Box 24, folder: U.S. Domestic Peace Corps (Proposal), CSWE Records, SWHA.

Wolfe, C. H. (1992). *Oral History by J. K. Parker*. Washington, DC: NASW.

6

Poverty, Public Welfare, and Professionalism
Opportunity Lost

GARY R. LOWE and P. NELSON REID

The idea of professionalization is a compelling one: Establish a body of knowledge specific to a crucial problem or process in society, create an educated and committed body of persons to apply that knowledge, and organize such application in publicly sanctioned contexts like schools, hospitals, and social agencies. This certainly seemed, to the educated American mind of the late nineteenth and early twentieth centuries, as the self-evident way to deal with many problems of society and the idea would be applied in medicine, engineering, nursing, and education. It would also be applied to social work, to the problems of poverty and dependence. Such professionalization would allow the development of a policy and practice for dealing with the poor and dependent based on rational, scientific processes and in so doing avoid the excesses of both politics and religion in approaching the problems of human need.

Early social work leadership placed a strong faith in such rationality and science, and understood it as the base for both professional identity and professional status. The desire for professional recognition greatly intensified as a result of Flexner's 1915 pronouncement of social work's failure to attain such status. Legitimacy and professional authority, as Flexner noted, involves the establishment of an identifiable body of formal knowledge, distinct in character and practice from other professions. Once a body of knowledge and practice is created, a profession must also establish a means to control its application and, of course, its applicants. Professional identity, public recognition, and possibly a measure of status and prestige, may well follow (cf. Freidson, 1986).

Professional status, of course, is not simply a matter of income or social status, it is about social authority: the authority to exercise professional judgment and to apply the knowledge and skill in which one is trained. It is about deference to that professional knowledge and the control of both information and the interpretation of information within a problem context. The apparent masters of such professionalism early in this century were, of course, those in medicine and it was to medicine that social work would look (cf. Flexner, 1915; Lubove, 1965; Ehrenreich, 1985; Lowe 1985, 1987), and look with a certain intensity, for as Ehrenreich (1985) observed, "[S]ocial work, perhaps more than any other major profession, has been obsessed with professional status" (p. 14).

That professional obsession would be made up of a combination of inequalities and inequities, involving both gender and a scientific bias against the social and psychological, and it would prove strong and enduring. But it would also come from a genuine inability to define precisely what social work is and does, and a genuine reluctance to accept a definition of its "clients" in terms of poverty and dependence. Despite the clear public mandate that social work received in the first decades of the century to be the profession responsible for the poor, the profession could not embrace this responsibility as central to its identity. Nowhere is this more evident than in the profession's struggle to control its professional education process and its rejection of undergraduate education and, by implication, public welfare as a site of professional practice.

THE FAILURE TO ORGANIZE A PROFESSION FOR THE POOR

While there are numerous forms of occupational control, a common aspect of professionalism[1] involves the control of entry into the educational process, and the subsequent regulation of the credentialing procedure and entry into the arena of practice. In this way the professional labor system is linked from admission to professional school through licensing and specialized certification to hiring, evaluation, continuing education, and management of professional standards (cf. Freidson, 1970a,b; Geison, 1983). The simple economics of professional supply and demand require that a profession not only control educational entry, but also establish an authoritative mechanism for control over placement and definition of demand. If unable to establish and maintain such control, a professional group may suffer from the intrusion of another professional group in its service arena as competitors or constraints on its ability to define its own work. Modern American medicine, once the envy of all other professional groups, is now regarded as relatively powerless in the face of managed care providers and competitive professional suppliers like nursing. These two are linked, of course, because as the pressure for cost control has increased, managed care both reduces the professional discretion of physicians and stimulates the search for lower cost labor to supply the needed services.

For social work the level of professional demand throughout the century has been generally high and the profession has been called upon to provide a sufficient supply of willing and professionally competent practitioners. In those circumstances where the supply has not been adequate, the demand has been met extraprofessionally, that is by hiring persons with no professional training and relying upon in-service education. Indeed, the historical record demonstrates that social work leadership refused to respond to obvious market demand at a critical point in American social service development, explaining its position as an effort to promote and protect professional standards in pursuit of an "ideal."[2]

Social work's pursuit of this professional ideal led to a failure to define its domain of activity and it was therefore unable to establish and protect its borders and to assert its professional authority in the context of services for the poor and dependent. Authority in this sense means the "surrender of private judgment" that is required in any professional/client transaction (Starr, 1982, p. 10). Given that social work, perhaps more than any other profession, involves the transfer of personal, family, and community lay decisions into the hands of "trained" professionals, the issue of authority is central to understanding social work's professional development. However, equally important is the "conversion" of authority into professional status and privilege (cf. Freidson, 1986). Starr (1982) notes that this conversion for medicine "required the medical profession to gain control over both the market for its services and the various organizational hierarchies that govern medical practice" (p. 21).

For medicine, this conversion of authority into an autonomous, high-status, well-paid professional practice came at a crucial time. Starr (1982) reminds us that earlier in this century insurance companies might have hired doctors to perform services for which beneficiaries were covered, and hospitals could have had salaried medical personnel to carry out all medical procedures. It was at this crucial time in the organization of hospitals and the earliest extensions of insurance into health care, both in response to increased demands for medical services, that the medical profession was able to exercise the sort of control that would help it remain autonomous for several more decades.

Social work, of course, never really established a professional practice outside the "salaried employee" of the agency model. Consequently the bulk of social work has been practiced not in market conditions with high accountability to the consumer, but in agency monopoly conditions, which limit both client and worker choice (cf. Reid, 1972). It needs to be emphasized here that the "monopoly" dimension was not a creation of social work, but of other agencies, most significantly the federal government during the 1930s. Further, social workers were central to the development and guidance of this emerging monopoly during the 1930s (cf. Chambers, 1963), but somehow failed to take full advantage of the opportunity (cf. Fisher, 1980).

That is, the federal government, while sponsoring the monopoly, turned to social work and offered it the opportunity to become its agent and to consolidate occupational control over the market. We maintain that social work refused to grasp the opportunity presented. Such an opportunity occurs to a profession during periods of rapid increase in demand for its services (cf. Selander, 1990). If the demand is sustained and the profession is either unable or unwilling to supply "certified" professional labor, it will suffer the certainty that the demand will be satisfied from elsewhere, possibly from undifferentiated and "noncertified" sources.

The most dramatic increase in demand for social service personnel in the United States occurred in the 1930s. Indications of this rapid rise in social service employment are readily cited: civilian employment in the federal government grew from less than 600,000 in 1930 to over 1,000,000 by 1940 (90% of this outside Washington D.C.). State and local employment in non-school related areas increased from 1.4 million in 1930 to about 4 million in 1938. It would not be until 1958 that another 600,000 employees would be added to the state and local governments.

Expenditures in government also increased rapidly during this period. Federal, state, and local public welfare costs increased from $400 million in 1930 to over $1.5 billion by 1940! It would take another twenty-two years, to 1962, before a tripling of expenditures in public welfare would occur again. In 1930, the U.S. Census counted 30,500 "social and welfare workers" but according to federal program data the Federal Emergency Relief Agency (FERA) alone employed over 60,000 in 1934. At the same time, the American Association of Social Workers (AASW), the main professional social work organization, enrolled only a small portion of these workers; 4,000 in 1930, doubling to 8,000 by 1934.

This was, by any account, an unprecedented opportunity for social work, an opportunity for which social work would have seemed well prepared. Its systems of credentials and education were in place and the profession seemed to have a legitimate and well-established claim to competence in the area of social service to the needy. Since the emergence of social work in the charity organizing movement in the late 1800s, the profession had held itself as having a special competence in regard to the management and prevention of dependence. It was an occupation primarily associated with the provision of assistance, of one kind or another, to the poor without damaging the larger interest of society. This was no light labor, and there were no competitive professions at the time claiming the same expertise! This last point is worth particular note since medicine was such an important model for social work, and medicine was in evident competition in its formative professional years with related occupations such as holistic practitioners, midwives, herbalists, and nurses. Thus not only did social work have an opportunity placed before it, but social work also had little or no competition for its claimed area of expertise.

However, for reasons having to do with status anxiety and an odd reluctance to claim its own skill in the area of demand, social work shied away. In so doing the profession failed to establish an effective monopoly over the emerging public welfare social service labor supply and that demand was subsequently filled from elsewhere. Social work's hesitation also created the foundation for a long-enduring "two-tiered" social work consisting, on the one hand, of a "low," public agency social work, unregulated and arguably unprofessional, and, on the other, of a "high" social work that would become concentrated in private agency settings. Perhaps most significantly, social work's reluctance to establish itself in the public welfare sector contributed immeasurably to a common public confusion of social work's technical and professional competence.

THE PUBLIC WELFARE DEBATE IN SOCIAL WORK

During the thirties, beginning with the creation of FERA and the subsequent passage of the Social Security Act (SSA), the rapidly expanding public welfare agencies sought aid and assistance from social work, to provide not only leadership, but also trained staff personnel.

Josephine C. Brown, the social worker who was the head of FERA, writing to Mildred Mudgett of the AASSW in May of 1934 stated that "there will be a larger number of students than schools can absorb and therefore we [FERA] will be in a position of passing upon special courses and field work facilities which are set up for the purpose . . . [of increasing the number of qualified personnel]" (CSWE, 1934). Public resources such as those referred to by Brown exemplified the continuing shift from private to public support for social welfare, which had occurred since the start of the depression and Roosevelt becoming president. For example, "In 1929 private sources still provided 25 percent of relief funds, as well as a host of non-relief services; by 1939 less than 1 percent of these funds were nongovernmental" (Ehrenreich, 1985, p. 106). In apparent response to Brown's note to the AASSW, a memorandum from "The Advisory Committee Appointed by the AASSW. . . . Regarding Training of Personnel for Federal Relief Service" recommended that "the establishment of new schools . . . or new training courses on Federal Relief funds should be avoided if possible" (CSWE, 1934). While the federal government was

exploring new approaches to public relief, and establishing new structures
to implement these approaches, the social work establishment was busy
attending to its long-standing quest for professional recognition and status. No clearer example of this exists than the policy adopted by the
AASSW in 1932, the darkest year of the depression, stating that "all professional education for social work was to be offered as graduate study
after October 1, 1936" (Hollis & Taylor, 1951, p. 29).

FERA was disbanded in 1935 as the way was made for the implementation of the Social Security Act and the beginning of the second New Deal.
At the 1935 National Conference of Social Work (NCSW), in a paper entitled "What We Have Learned About Emergency Training for Public Relief
Administration," Sophonisba Breckinridge of the University of Chicago
reviewed the FERA experience and in the process restated and reinforced
the casework ideology and the high educational standard that had taken
shape as "graduate only" entry to the profession. Breckinridge, reflecting
the continuing atomistic/adjustment notions grounded in the casework
perspective, stated that "the successful treatment of destitution involves
not only the supply of adequate relief at that time, but such readjustment
of individual to environment as eliminates a recurrence of the condition"
(*Proceedings*, 1935, p. 247). After restating the basic Flexnerian ideal trait
perspective on professions, Breckinridge offered the generic rational for
even higher educational standards by observing that "no profession or calling can rise above the general level of its educational standard" (p. 248).

Throughout the thirties, the AASW had struggled with issues of membership definition, and this led to tension between it and the educational
association (AASSW) since the latter was continually pushing for even
higher standards. The dilemma facing the AASW was how to maintain a
reasonable membership base given the increasing numbers of persons
entering social work type positions and also the wish to support AASSW's
efforts to raise the standards of the profession.[3] Commenting on these tensions, Breckinridge, chiding the professional association, further noted
that within the context of "emergency" "the practicing group (AASW)
acknowledges the importance of professional education but is sometimes
unable to contemplate the sacrifices necessary to secure a sound basis" (p.
250). Breckinridge's mention of sacrifices referred to the need to limit
membership only to those with proper credentials. All of these comments
by Breckinridge were cogent reminders that in spite of the current emergency, social work educational leadership was still committed to reinforc-
ing "high standards." At the time, 1935, at least one year of graduate study
was established as the minimum norm for "professional education."

In order to place Breckinridge's comments in perspective, one needs to
be reminded that in the same year of this speech, FERA alone employed
60,000 persons, while the total nationwide AASW membership numbered

approximately 8,000 and the nationwide enrollment in the various schools of social work numbered somewhere in the vicinity of 6,600 students in the thirty recognized schools of social work. Of these students, 2,712 were full time, 2,547 were part-time, and 1,343 "were at least taking courses" (Breckinridge, 1935, p. 250). Two years later, at the 1937 NCSW, Walter West, executive secretary of the AASW, in a paper titled "Purpose and Value of Standards in Social Work," echoed Breckinridge specifically in the area of educational standards "[S]tandards would, if they were possible, straighten out many of the complications by which social work is made confusing to the public, and to ourselves. . . . [I]t may be conceded that it is of great importance in dealing with human problems as social work does, that such standards should be the highest obtainable" (p. 2). West and Breckinridge's comments reflect the continuing emphasis during the 1930s on profession building rather than public service, communicating a growing ambivalent public welfare commitment.

At midyear in 1937, a report titled "The Problem of Pre-Requisites for Admissions to Schools of Social Work" was released by the Curriculum Committee of the AASSW. This report recommended "[t]hat beginning October 1, 1939, such instruction as is given on an undergraduate level be treated as pre-professional" (Browning and Houk, AASSW, 1937, p. 7). The rationale supporting this recommendation was at best ironic and reflected the continued high standards orthodoxy and its continuing power driving professional education policy:

> The conception of the scope, and perhaps the content, of social work is changing rapidly. The term, social work, was a few years ago largely identified with social case-work; some group work, but what came to be called "public welfare work" was for a period of years almost ruled out. . . . Social work was par excellence private social case-work, medical social work, psychiatric social work, etc. Experience with relief during the Depression and the passage of the Federal Social Security Act have elevated public welfare work and social insurance to the dominant place in the field of social welfare activities. (p. 5)

Indeed public welfare had become "dominant" in American social welfare, but given the limited number of graduate schools and graduate students it is puzzling how the graduate-only policy could possibly be reconciled with the real demand for social work practitioners.

With the ultimate passage of the SSA, and the devolution of many relief activities to local jurisdiction, pressure again increased to provide "qualified" personnel at the local level. With this shift from federally mandated relief efforts to locally based services, by the close of the 1930s the public welfare protagonists were no longer social work leaders debating "up" to the federal level; instead those in AASW and AASSW found themselves facing "down" to the state and local levels. With positions such as those articulated in 1937 by the AASSW Curriculum Committee regarding public welfare and graduate education, the 1940s witnessed the emergence of a significant cast of new protagonists, specifically state institutions of higher education.

The 1940s were marked by a reescalation of the status vs. market debate and conflict within social work. In reaction those committed to public welfare advocated the recognition of a role for the undergraduate- prepared social worker as a means of providing larger numbers of trained line workers. This would enhance, not detract from, social work professionalization, they argued. These forces coalesced into a group called the National Association of Schools of Social Administration (NASSA). NASSA's purpose was "to promote instruction in the social services on as broad and as flexible a basis as is commensurate with sound educational policy" (CSWE, 1944). Arrayed against NASSA was the established, orthodox social work leadership digging in its heels, strongly and stubbornly continuing to insist on a high-status orientation to professional development.

NASSA, though never very large, managed to bring together individuals and institutions who were both frustrated and alienated by AASSW's real and perceived high-handed elitist pursuit of graduate-only professional education. The pressure exerted by NASSA, particularly on some of the larger land grant and other state universities, was perceived as significant by AASSW. Evidence of this can be found in a letter dated January 29, 1944, sent to Gordon Hamilton, President of the AASSW, and written by F. Stuart Chapin, then head of the AASSW's Advisory Committee on State Universities and Membership Requirement. Written in a scrawled hand on Hotel Lincoln (Indianapolis, Indiana) stationary, Chapin observed:

> [Y]ou might as well face the following facts which show a convergence and adhesion menacing in the extreme to the standards of the entire AASSW. . . . [T]the support for the new Association [NASSA] stems from the most powerful (quite beyond the conception and realization of most members of the AASSW) combine of institutions of higher education in the country. (CSWE, 1944)

NASSA's efforts developed throughout the 1940s to the point where AASSW had to respond to the growing threat, most specifically in the area of accrediting professional educational programs. In NASSA, the AASSW and AASW had a genuine threat to its professionalizing efforts. Ironically, the perceived threat was not from outside the occupation, but from within its own ranks and consisted of educators who also understood and valued standards.[4]

One response to NASSA by the AASSW was to form a joint committee on accrediting in an effort to engage the rival association in discussion and dialogue. In 1947, Chancellor R. G. Gustavson of the University of Nebraska was about to assume the chair of the Joint (AASSW/NASSA) Committee on Accrediting. Dr. Frank Glick, then director of the School of Social Work at Nebraska, in correspondence providing background of the struggle to his chancellor, articulated a useful and, given the nature of the struggle of the time, very reasoned and balanced overview of the history leading to the tensions in the social work field:

> The real strength and quality of professional instruction in our field, in terms of both institution and personnel, is in the AASSW. Personnel standards of government and voluntary agencies which employ trained social workers are based on training accredited by AASSW. . . . It holds staunchly to the position, which I share, that a thoroughly competent professional social worker cannot be produced in less than two years of hard work on top of a good liberal education. . . . Great expansion of the public social services since the 1930s has created thousands of social work positions in the country which are very modestly compensated but which need people with some training for the job. The only feasible answer the universities could give to this personnel shortage was to offer some undergraduate training. AASSW schools pretty rigidly refused to do this, which really meant sticking their heads in the sand. . . . This situation gave birth to NASSA. . . . NASSA has achieved very little status in the social work world. . . . But if it does nothing more, it has served as a catalyst in the whole business of education for social work. (CSWE, NASSA vs. AASSW, Box 15)

As midcentury approached, the two factions slowly moved toward a well-established social work education problem-solving method: the initiation of a major curriculum study/review. Therefore, in 1950, the Hollis/Taylor Study was begun in the hopes of settling the divisive issues.[5] The study process was not without its own controversy, with NASSA particularly concerned that the process not be skewed too heavily against its cause and the AASSW was concerned that the long struggle for standards not be undercut. Once the Hollis/Taylor study was published (1951), its basic thrust seemed to be a reaffirmation of the graduate-only position. The report itself provided only lukewarm support for undergraduate preparation by acknowledging a somewhat nonspecific "continuum" between undergraduate social work and graduate preparation. Further, Hollis/Taylor specifically called for the dropping of "preprofessional" as a label for those existing social work undergraduate programs.

In spite of the fundamental reaffirmation of the graduate-only position by Hollis/Taylor, the surrounding social work practice context had not changed and the need for large numbers of professionally trained public welfare social workers continued to go unmet. That is, while the AASSW had been successful in reasserting its push for a high-standard professional model, this thrust was completely in contradiction to the continuing and growing demand in the public welfare sector. For example, by 1950

roughly 84 percent of all those in the United States defined as having social
work roles were, in effect, nonprofessional by social work's own definition
(having an MSW). Fifty-seven percent of all social workers were in some
public welfare role including public assistance and child welfare and of
the 40 percent (30,110) involved in public assistance, only 4 percent had
two or more years of graduate social work education (U.S. Dept. of Labor
Statistics, 1950).

A specific outcome of Hollis/Taylor was the formation of the Council
on Social Work Education (CSWE) in 1952, combining the various competing professional educational organizations. Undergraduate proponents were submerged in the new CSWE as only an interest section. In
effect, the high- standard advocates had reestablished their position. Nevertheless, demand continued to grow for differentiated social work personnel other than those being squeezed into and out of the narrow channel
of graduate education. In less than a decade following Hollis/Taylor and
CSWE's creation, with the advent of new Social Security amendments in
the 1960s, the issue of social work's public welfare role would again be
revisited when the federal government would, as it had in the first New
Deal, articulate a very real public welfare personnel need requiring social
work to respond. The result of this external demand and other pressures
internal to the profession (e.g., the *Curriculum Study* of 1959/1960) was
that social work finally responded by incorporating undergraduate education (1974) as entry level, and in this way social work finally placed itself
in a position potentially to control supply (cf. Selandar, 1990; Brante,
1990).

THE MYTH OF PROFESSIONAL COMMITMENT

Using evidence from the 1930s and 1940s, we have seen that the leaders
of professional social work sacrificed extensive professional involvement
and presence in public social services for the poor as a means to establish
a professional identity and acceptance for the profession. The leaders of
the profession did not act out of concern for the quality of service provided
in public agencies nor on the basis of an apparent need to control an occupational domain. Instead, they pursued a model of social work professionalization based upon an ideal of postbaccalaureate preparation.
Ironically as a result, these actions undermined the very object they
intended to attain: the achievement of full professional status, professional
authority, and effective monopoly.

In the 1930s and 1940s, when market demand was expanding at
unprecedented rates, social work did exactly the opposite of what would
have been expected had the leadership understood and acted on the basis

of market supply and demand dynamics. Had the leadership of social work acted on the basis of an understanding of these market principles, it would have adopted a strategy that would have expanded market supply sufficiently and consolidated control over the organization, definition, and evaluation of social work practice (cf. Freidson, 1970a). Instead, social work leadership acted to reduce legitimate supply by insisting on professional education as "graduate" education, at a time when schools of social work could not keep pace with demand. In addition, this same leadership discouraged the use of federal funds for the expansion and establishment of schools and training programs. These actions by the leadership contributed to an unstable market situation and ensured that the demand for line social work staff, particularly in the public welfare arena, would have to be met extraprofessionally.

As a result of these historical actions, social work has had difficulty establishing effective boundaries and meaningful occupational control over its maximum realm of activity. The particular outcome of the situation asserted above can be stated in the following way:

The professional status model historically pursued by social work, rather than securing occupational control over its relevant field of activity, has been divisive and has undermined, perhaps irreparably, the achievement of full professional maturity.

We think one of the most significant historical actions taken by social work that contributed to its division as an occupation was the adoption of a *graduate-only* educational model, during the 1930s as both entry-level as well as terminal professional certification (Lowe, 1985; Leighninger, 1984). This educational policy decision had two immediate consequences for social work, which continue to exert influence in important ways to the present:

1. From an ideological perspective, the graduate-only educational stance, with its direct link to the casework method, blinded social work to the immediate relevance and continuing importance of the demand in the broad public social welfare sector below the supervisory, administrative level.

2. On the practical side, the graduate-only model assured social work's inability to provide a sufficient supply of trained personnel for the rapidly expanding demand in the public social welfare sector.

As a result of social work's inability or unwillingness to respond to the increasing demand for social work trained personnel, virtually all public welfare personnel, prior to 1974, were untrained professionally and what little training they possessed was not in social welfare/work–related areas, since the only recognized (by social work itself, AASW) preparation for the field increasingly existed at the graduate level and was generally unavailable and probably irrelevant to the nature of the growing local public social welfare delivery needs (Maxted, 1945).

The result of the above historical process has been paradoxical. Specifically, a central outcome of the creation of institutional public social welfare through the New Deal resulted in the public coming to view social work's primary function to be in the area of public social welfare, but social work itself was consciously moving in a direction of standard setting that would virtually cut its ties with the public welfare sector.

Historically, social work has been ambivalent at best in regards to public social welfare as a realm of professional activity. This ambivalence has been reframed in social workers' collective consciousness and has attained the place of a positive myth. We now invoke what was once a very uncomfortable (at best) public welfare role as a positive image of some lost but important past or as confused history of the profession's legacy (Specht & Courtney, 1994). Ironically, this myth is offered in the face, not only of a counterhistorical record, but also with increasing evidence that a commitment to public welfare is not a driving motivation for future social workers, particularly those persons entering MSW programs (Rubin & Anderson, 1984). Therefore, what is not recognized or understood by many who assert this myth is that the current manifestation of a low public welfare commitment on the part of future social workers emerges, not as something new and aberrant or symptomatic of a lingering 1980s "me" yuppie phenomenon, but is simply the most recent expression of a rich and long-standing tradition in social work, which has shunned a meaningful role in the public welfare sector.

In conclusion, we return to the midcentury struggle between AASSW and NASSA for our closing thought. On the eve of the creation of the Council on Social Work Education (CSWE), which incorporated both associations, Professor Mattie Cal Maxted of the University of Arkansas and the last NASSA president pinpointed the consequences of social work's refusal to understand the professional relevance of the public welfare demand and the importance of providing an adequate supply of professionally prepared personnel. Her words ring with a disturbing relevance some forty years later:

> The social work profession is not facing up to the fact that thousands of social work positions are now, and will continue to be for a long time, filled by persons without graduate education in social work. . . . [T]here are a hundred of these so-called social workers to every trained one. Thus, it is the untrained ones who are molding public opinion as to the nature of social work, and attitudes towards the profession are in danger of becoming crystallized in the public mind by the standards set by these unprepared workers. (Maxted, 1952)

NOTES

1. Unionization is another form of occupational control social work could have adopted, but given the general class backgrounds of much of the social work leadership of the time and a general atmosphere not favorable to unions, one can see why this option would not have offered itself as attractive.

2. The "ideal," or trait notion of a profession as articulated by Flexner in 1915 contained six key points that he stated must be present in order to have a legitimate profession: (1) intellectual operations; (2) scientific learning base; (3) practical and definite ends; (4) educationally communicable techniques; (5) self-organization, and (6) altruistic motivation.

3. AASW struggled throughout the 1930s to establish membership guidelines, which would provide support to the educator's goals of higher and rising standards while also striving to bring in new members. This struggle to serve these two often opposing ends was addressed in Section 6 of AASW's membership requirements: "The Executive Committee may in exceptional circumstances elect to membership persons who do not technically meet the requirements [set out by the other association membership rules]" (NASW/AASW, 1930–1953). In a report to the board of directors of AASW by the National Membership Committee (October 9, 1942), the following statement was made as to the purpose of Section 6: "Enlarging the membership of the association so that its influence could be quantitatively greater and its membership more genuinely representative of the large numbers of people taken into social work positions during the rapid period of expansion of public social service in the 30s" (NASW/AASW, 1930–1953).

4. The rank-and-file movement is the oft-cited instance of genuine threat to social work as it struggled to establish professional standards. While the rank-and-file movement was perceived as a threat at a critical developmental period, its existence was rather short-lived and its impact minimal. In addition, the majority of those who were rank-and-file advocates were viewed as existing on the profession's edge. NASSA, on the other hand, was comprised of established, even orthodox fellow educators. Further, NASSA's demands symbolized a transformation in the nature of the profession as it had been developing.

5. Prior to Hollis/Taylor, social work had conducted three other studies: (1) James H. Tufts, *Education and Training for Social Work* (1923); (2) Paul Beisser, "A Measurement of Professional Training: Deductions from a Questionnaire Study of Social Work Positions" (1923); and (3) James E. Hagerty, *The Training of Social Workers* (1931). Following Hollis/Taylor, in 1959, the so-called *Curriculum Study* was completed. This massive study articulated a clear place for undergraduate education and was instrumental in finally moving the profession toward the recognition and incorporation of this level of preparation as entry-level professional, (cf. Bisno, 1959).

REFERENCES

Beisser, Paul (1923). A measurement of professional training. *Compass, 3* (February 23, Supplement), p. 3–6.

Bisno, Herbert (1959). *The Place of the Undergraduate Curriculum in Social Work Education*. New York: Council on Social Work Education.

Boehm, Werner W. 1959. *Objective for the Social Work Curriculum of the Future* (Vols. 1–13). New York: CSWE.

Brante, Thomas (1990). Professional types as a strategy of analysis. In Michael Burrage and Rolf Torstendahl (Eds.), *Professions in Theory and History* (pp. 75–93). London: Sage.

Breckinridge, S. (1935). What we have learned about emergency training for public relief administration. *Proceedings, National Conference on Social Work* (pp. 246–258). Chicago: University of Chicago Press.

Browning, X ., and Houk, X . (1937). *AASSW, 1935–1943*. Minneapolis, MN: Social Work Archives.

Burrage, Michael (1990). Introduction: The professions in sociology and history. In Michael Burrage and Rolf Torstendahl (Eds.), *Professions in Theory and History* (pp. 1–23). London: Sage.

Chambers, Clarke (1963). *Seedtime for Reform*. Minneapolis: University of Minnesota Press.

CSWE (1944). "NASSA vs. CSWE." Box 15, 1944, Social Welfare History Archives, University of Minnesota Libraries, Minneapolis.

Ehrenreich, John H. (1985). *The Altruistic Imagination: A History of Social Work and Social Policy in the United States*. Ithaca, NY: Cornell University Press.

Fisher, J. (1980). *The Response of Social Work to the Depression*. Boston, Hall.

Flexner, Abraham (1915). Is social work a profession? In *Proceedings of the National Conference of Charities and Corrections* (pp. 576–590). Chicago: Hillman.

Freidson, Eliot (1970a). *Professional Dominance: The Social Structure of Medical Care*. New York: Atherton.

Freidson, Eliot (1970b). *Profession of Medicine: A Study of the Sociology of Applied Knowledge*. New York: Harper and Row.

Freidson, Eliot (1986). *Professional Powers: A Study of the Institutionalization of Former Knowledge*. Chicago: University of Chicago Press.

Geison, Gerald L. (1983). Introduction. In Gerald L. Geison (Ed.), *Professions and Professional Ideologies in America* (pp. 3–11). Chapel Hill: University of North Carolina Press.

Hagerty, James H. (1931). *The Training of Social Workers*. New York: Mcgraw Hill.

Hollis, Ernest V., & Taylor, Alice L. (1951). *Social Work in the United States*. New York: Columbia University Press.

Leighninger, Leslie (1984). Graduate and undergraduate social work education: Roots of conflict. *Journal of Education for Social Work, 20*(3), 66–77.

Lowe, Gary (1985). The graduate-only debate in social work education 1931–1959, and its consequences for the profession. *Journal of Education for Social Work* (Winter):52–62.

Lowe, Gary (1987). Social work's professional mistake: Confusing status for control and losing both. *Sociology and Social Welfare, 14*(2, June), 187–206.

Lubove, Roy (1965). *The Professional Altruist: The Emergence of Social Work as a Career 1880–1930*. Cambridge, MA: Harvard University Press.

Maxted Collection (1945). "The Need for Undergraduate Trained Social Workers in Arkansas." Mimeograph, Social Welfare History Archives, University of Minnesota Libraries, Minneapolis.

Maxted Collection (1952). "Undergraduate Social Work Education: Stepchild or Baby?" Mimeograph, Social Welfare History Archives, University of Minnesota Libraries, Minneapolis.

NASW/AASW, "Membership Committee: Regulations and Requirements, 1930–1953." Box 6, folder 57.

Reid, P. Nelson (1972). Reforming the social service monopoly. *Social Work, 16,* 44–54.

Rubin, A., & Johnson, P. J. (1984). Direct practice interests of entering msw students. *Journal of Education for Social Work, 20,* 15–16.

Rubin, A., Johnson, P. J., & DeWeaver, Kevin L. (1986). Direct practice interests of msw students: changes from entry to graduation. *Journal of Education for Social Work, 22,* 98–108.

Selander, Staffan (1990). Associative strategies in the process of professionalization: professional strategies and scientification of occupation. Michael Burrage and Rolf Torstendahl (Eds.), *Professions in Theory and History* (pp. 139–150). London: Sage.

Specht, Harry & Courtney, Mark (1994). *Unfaithful Angels: How Social Work Has Abandoned Its Mission.* New York: Free Press.

Starr, Paul (1982). *The Social Transformation of American Medicine.* New York: Basic Books.

Tufts, James H. (1923). *Education and Training for Social Workers.* New York: Russell Sage Foundation.

U.S. Department of Labor Statistics (1950). *Social Workers in 1950.* Washington, DC: Bureau of Labor Statistics, Division of Wages and Industrial Relations.

7

"Prising Open That Old Prejudiced Door"
African-Americans, Poverty, and Social Work in the Early Twentieth Century

SUSAN KERR CHANDLER

You sang:
Ain't no hammah
in dis lan', bebby
Strikes lak mine, bebby,
Strikes lak mine.

They cooped you in their kitchens,
They penned you in their factories,
They gave you the jobs that they were too good for,
They tried to guarantee happiness to themselves
By shunting dirt and misery on to you.

You sang:
Me an' muh baby gonna shine, shine,
Me an' muh baby gonna shine.

The strong men keep a-comin' on . . .

Sterling Brown, *Strong Men*

During the first two, incredible decades of this century, in the years when social work was establishing itself and its reason for being, social workers were often drawn to work with poor and laboring people. They took positions in the thick of it, in the expansive, loud, industrial cities where immigrants, people from small towns and farms, and black southerners arrived daily in search of jobs and a more hopeful future. Differing greatly in both philosophy and method of work, many social workers nevertheless united around the notion that their work should be with the poor. Thus, charity workers made friendly visits, settlement house residents moved into immigrant neighborhoods, activists pressed for protective legislation, black professionals labored to move African-Americans out of the south, and welfare secretaries in factories sought to create a new, social hygiene of industry. A number of leading social workers, Jane Addams and Florence Kelley among them, had grown up in families with strong Abolitionist traditions and had more than passing familiarity with socialism, internationalism, and trade unionism. World citizens, they were determined to participate in the building of a responsible public polity. These social work pioneers, heroes of the profession, are not particularly representative of social workers today, but their role as defenders of the poor remains central to social work's identity.

Why didn't social work's intensive involvement with workers and the poor last? And how is it that the convictions of women like Jane Addams are strong enough to inspire the profession at the millennium, yet clearly failed to carry the day during most of this century? This chapter suggests that racial privilege and segregation in social services during the first four decades of the century, and white social work's unwillingness to fight them, are part of the answer to that question. Taking the perspective of African-American workers and professionals during this period of enormous change along the color line, the chapter argues that white social work's decision to work within segregated social service programs absolutely compromised the profession's ability to address issues of poverty, isolated it from activists and scholars within the black community, contributed to the ascendancy of a narrow, apolitical vision in the profession, and led to the deeply ambivalent feeling about social work found among African- Americans and other oppressed people even today.

Ida B. Wells-Barnett, the great activist and crusader against lynching, shocked a white audience in a 1908 speech in Chicago by spelling out what was common knowledge for African-Americans in that city: "that Chicagoans could enter the settlements, YMCAs, YWCAs and every other movement for uplift . . . if only their skins are white." "The occasional black man who wanders uninvited into these places," Mrs. Wells-Barnett went on, "is very quickly given to understand that his room is better than his company." Later that evening a white woman came up to Mrs. Wells-Barnett and asked if she had understood her correctly to say that the YMCA did not admit black men. "I assured her that . . . it was a fact," Wells-Barnett remembered, to which the woman replied, "I am so surprised to hear this. I am sure my husband does not know it and only last year he gave several thousand dollars to that organization" (Duster, 1970, pp. 301–302).

Racial privilege and racial segregation were basic organizing principles of U.S. social services during the first four decades of the century. While philanthropists like the surprised Chicago couple and most white social workers would have been chagrined to have the matter put so bluntly, African-Americans were intimately familiar with the color line in social services and could have offered countless examples of its effect.

In the South, black observers would have pointed out, the chance that a black southerner might have a helpful encounter with a white social worker was laughably small. Who among white professionals made themselves familiar with the desperate poverty of those years and how close to the edge most African-Americans lived? Which white social worker spoke boldly—or at all—at local and national conferences about the starvation of the black South? No article or speech may be found, and yet the realities were plainly visible. A Louisiana woman, in one of hundreds of letters black southerners wrote to the *Defender,* Chicago's African-American newspaper, described her family's life of terror and privation: "My heart is upset night and day," she wrote, " . . . we are working people but we cant hardly live here I would say more but we are back in the jungles and we have to lie low" (Scott, 1919, p. 426). "I wish to say that we are forced to go [north]," a black minister wrote, "when one thinks of a grown mans wages is only fifty to seventy five cents per day. . . . [W]hen I say that many places here in this state the only thing that the black man gets is a peck of meal and from three to four lbs. of bacon per week, and he is treated as a slave. As leaders we are powerless for we dare not present such or to show even the slightest disapproval" (ibid., p. 451). In every community, black southerners secretly sought out information about the possibility of jobs and a new life in the north, where industrialists were desperate for workers to fill wartime factories. "Is there any wheare up there that I can get in with an intucion that I may get my wife and mysilf from down hear and can bring just as miney more as he want?" asked one of the hundreds of thousands of migrants who pressed against the system's limits. "I am a man hunting work," another wrote, "Please send the names of some firms that wants labor I am a Man who Beleave in right and Beleave in work and has worked all of my days and mean to work until I die and Never been No kind of trouble" (ibid., p. 296).

Two rules seemed to African-Americans to define the color line in social services: first, public and private relief for black Americans would be denied entirely or delivered in small, mean-spirited portions; and second, the provision of services would occur on a strictly segregated basis so that no white client would be offended by contact with African- Americans. In the South, particularly in the rural areas where poverty was most intense, there were generally no social services at all. Taxes, black and white, supported the building of a rudimentary system of services for white children, the aged, the blind, and others in need. African-American communities desiring social services, however, were compelled to fund and organize them themselves. In Atlanta, for example, the women of the Neighbor-hood Union, organized in 1908 by Eugenia Hope, created kindergartens for children of working mothers, conducted health and school surveys, and eventually were responsible for most of the social welfare work on Atlanta's west side (Shivery, 1936). On the critical issue of support for fam-ilies making the move north, black social service professionals, as we shall see later, were both passionate and active. The white profession, however, not only distanced itself from migrants, but denigrated "Northern enthu-siasts," and came down solidly on the side of the South's economic power brokers, who were determined to keep black workers in the South (Weath-erford, 1911).

It was not only in the South, however, that race privilege in social ser-vices flourished. African-Americans who enlisted or were drafted into the armed services in 1917 and fought to make the world safe for democracy were enraged to witness the American command's effort to build a Jim-Crowed army with Jim-Crowed services on French soil (Chandler, 1995). The nearly two hundred thousand young black men who served overseas did not quickly forget the Whites Only signs on YMCA huts, and stories of ill-treatment were widely circulated in the black community, which closely followed the experiences of their boys in France. Eighty-five African-American social service professionals were recruited to staff a limited number of "colored" YMCA huts, and frequently wrote friends, families, and newspapers of their experience with the French, on the one hand—"so whole-souled and congenial!"—and their frustration with the YMCA offi-cials, on the other (Hunton & Johnson, 1920). Secretary A. S. Peal wrote after many days of watching almost all the supplies being claimed for white huts: "A complete YMCA outfit for our men will be probably the hardest thing to secure." He guessed that "preachment" and cigarettes could be acquired in adequate supply, but equipment and full programs for social, educational, and physical development would remain "quite scarce" (Peal, 1918). African-American soldiers and social service profes-sionals alike, bitterly disillusioned by the raw, racist behavior they encountered, worked passionately to build programs that dignified the young black men's service to their country. They emerged from war with a confidence, race pride, and anger that bolstered their challenges to inequality and segregation at home.

In the North, migrating African-Americans found as soon as they stepped off the southern trains that the color line in social services was sharply drawn there also. In the depots, Travelers Aid, the agency that had provided invaluable help to thousands of immigrants from Europe, kept its doors closed to African-Americans. Black migrants did not fail to note either that white settlements like Hull House did not welcome them, and that swimming pools in YMCAs and YWCAs elicited the same abhorrence of "intimate" contact with African-Americans that eating together had in the South. Even the most progressive settlement workers like Jane Addams, Louise de Koven, and Florence Kelley, who were generally much in advance of others in the profession in calling for racial justice, did not approve of "social equality," meaning open social interaction between black and white in eating, lodging, and, of course, in marriage (see Grossman, 1989; Philpott, 1978).

African-Americans watched carefully as northern liberals constructed a two-dimensional solution to the question of services for the rapidly expanding black population. First, in *public* agencies, where discrimination was forbidden by law, African-Americans would be directed away from central agencies and toward black branches "conveniently located" in the black ghetto or, occasionally, be served separately in the central office. Second, in *private* agencies, which provided the bulk of services, discrimination would be encouraged. African-American clients would be served only by "colored" agencies and white clients would be served only by white agencies. In both private and public settings, African-American social workers, generally carefully monitored by white supervisors, handled the "negro cases" and only the "negro cases." Regulatory boards and study commissions like Chicago's Commission on Race Relations, which was dominated by white social workers, encouraged the African-Americans to build their own settlements and services. They did not censure white settlements for refusing to accept blacks, nor did they challenge segregation, especially the grievous barriers in housing (see Philpott, 1978; Grossman, 1989).

Thus, in Pittsburgh, the Urban League successfully pushed the Public Health Nursing Association and Associated Charities to hire two black nurses and two "colored workers," respectively. Travelers Aid, too, was convinced to appoint a "colored worker" who "rendered definite service to more than 1,100 Negro travelers" that arrived at the Pittsburgh depot during the first six months of 1923 (Clark, 1923). On the other hand, private agencies like the Chicago Prairie Club, which promoted outdoor activities, advertised openly that its programs were "open to white people of any nationality or creed" (quoted in Philpott, 1978, p. 307). The great racial unrest of 1919 prompted reform movements in social services in cities like Chicago, but these movements had their limits as well, the most essential of which was that the system of segregation should remain intact. "Better services" thus meant better segregated services. "Better neighborhoods" meant not the opening of ghetto boundaries, but funds for a black settlement house—funds that predictably dried up as memories of racial unrest waned (see Philpott, 1978). Thus in black communities an officially sanctioned, inadequately funded, and continually neglected system of segregated public and private services functioned to provide minimal assistance to African-Americans and, at the same time, to veil the larger neglect.

Philanthropy, on which all private social service agencies were dependent, actively promoted segregation. In 1912 Julius Rosenwald, the owner of Sears and Roebucks and the U.S. philanthropist who most generously supported African-American programs, pledged $25,000 to any city that could raise $75,000 for a new, high-quality YMCA for "colored men and boys" (Washington, 1914). While the money was appreciated and resulted in the construction of twenty-five "colored Ys," black communities did not fail to note its tie to segregated facilities. W. E. B. Du Bois wrote in 1914, "The YMCA movement in America is not acting in a Christian manner toward colored folk. In most cities colored people are . . . excluded from all the well-equipped branches of the YMCA and herded in a poorly equipped 'colored' branch. . . . [The splendid new accommodations are] a fine thing . . . but it is an unchristian and unjust and dangerous procedure which segregates colored people in the YMCA movement" (1914).

Moreover, access to philanthropic funds was carefully reserved to white leaders or "responsible and reliable" African-American individuals and organizations. E. Franklin Frazier, the first director of the Atlanta University School of Social Work, was one of those "unreliable" persons who was unable to accept the "conditions of racial adjustment." He refused to attended segregated social work meetings and persisted in raising the question of segregation. His good friend, the satirist Gustavus Adolphus Steward, laughed at Frazier the summer after he was asked to resign his position at the Atlanta school for failing "once again" to "get back into the uplift and good graces of the philanthropic trust" (1927). Frazier later described the obligatory knuckling-under that was demanded of black agencies: "It has not been necessary, of course, for the foundations to make explicit demands upon the Negro teacher or intellectual [for everyone] realized that if he were to secure employment, he must indicate that his ideas of racial adjustment conformed to the social philosophy of the foundations" (1957, pp. 96–97).

Finally, the social work profession itself made it difficult for young African-Americans to acquire a social work education, secure jobs, and take on leadership within the larger social service community. Social work was an attractive option to young African-Americans seeking to be of service to their community and wishing a more secular approach to service than the ministry offered. But many were ambivalent about the profession, seeing opportunity for useful work, certainly, but aware at the same time of the segregation and control that characterized the profession's relations with its black members. The first black school of social work, the Atlanta University School, was not organized until 1921, and then only after black delegates led by Jesse O. Thomas, a black social work leader from Atlanta, protested the segregation of the New Orleans meeting of the National Conference of Social Work and called for the founding of a black school (Thomas, 1967, p. 117). The New York School of Philanthropy admitted one or two black students annually, as did the University of Pittsburgh and the University of Chicago, but segregated dormitories, libraries, and other facilities at most white schools effectively discouraged black students. Black social workers, with and without degrees, could routinely expect to be treated rudely, embarrassed, undermined, excluded from policymaking boards, overridden by white "experts on Negro affairs," and paid substantially less. In the YMCA, for example, black social service professionals in 1922 were paid on average, $2,537; whites, $3,959 ("Average Salaries" no date; Grossman, 1989). In a famous example, Robert Russa Moton, the distinguished president of Tuskegee Institute, was embarrassed when correspondence was uncovered in which one YMCA official wrote another that it would be "quite impossible to have [Moton]" at the luncheon of an important Washington, D.C., conference. The official suggested that President Moton, who had been invited to address a gathering of YMCA leaders, might be "accommodated behind a screen" in the hotel's segregated dining room and should be encouraged to seek lodging with his friends in the city, as he could not stay at the conference hotel (Cooper, 1923). Moton, when approached with this solution, replied with dignity, "I have reached the conclusion that it will be best all round that I do not attend this meeting. . . . When it comes to the place . . . where I must approach my friends with the apologies [you] suggest, I am moved to the conclusion that the persistence of such a situation can no longer be supported without compromising the Christian principles of all of us who may be party to it" (1923).

Black professionals especially resented white administrators' efforts to control them and to link black professionals with "good white people" in opposition to the "backward" or "radical elements" of the race, as the language of the day put it. Historian Carter G. Woodson in a 1932 column in the *New York Age* wrote in his characteristically sharp tone:

> For more than three generations the Negroes of this country have been bowing and kowtowing for a few thousand dollars obtained here and there, and they have not advanced toward the promised land which the self-chosen white leaders have pointed out. If you have to keep your mouth closed when it is time to speak out, if you have to subject your will to that of another to be sure of the geegaws and toys of life, you had just as well count on final re-enslavement.

Segregation and meanness of spirit in the provision of social services was scarcely an accident or remnant of a former period of history, but proceeded directly from closely held early twentieth-century public and professional worldviews. African-American professionals were all too familiar with these patterns of thought. South and North, a suffocating liberal paternalism provided the dominant context within which services for African-Americans were seen, and underlay a series of theories and attitudes. Among these were the beliefs (1) that "efficiency" (that is, hard, work, cleanliness, and loyalty) was central to black advancement and (2) that African-Americans should be grateful for services and not demand them.

Weatherford, a southern "expert on racial affairs," articulated liberal paternalism well in his text *Negro Life in the South*, in which he described a "commitment to the negro" thoroughly laced with deep-rooted beliefs of black inferiority. Weatherford urged white men to "study the Negro," so that *"we will be able so to deal with these weaker peoples as to prove to God and to the world that we are a race of superior advancement* . . . . It is just because the negro is ignorant" [emphasis in the original].

Weatherford continued, "just because he is having a hard battle to win industrial competence; just because he is sinking under the burdens of awful diseases and just because he has not yet attained unto the full stature of moral manhood" that southern white men, who "love our homes and want to protect them," must "lend a helping hand to the race that is down" (1911, pp. 20–21; Brown, 1919; Wilson, 1925).

Weatherford went on to elaborate a theory of the "best white men" and the "better class of negroes" working together toward racial adjustment and in opposition to the classes of men who had "fueled the fires" of racial discord. These latter classes included the Prejudiced Southern White Man (the so-called defenders of the white man's honor and the white woman's virtue); the Radical Negro (the "Niagara movement, W. E. B. Du Bois, . . . men who see no virtue in the southern white man"), and the Northern Enthusiast (1911, pp. 11–12). Weatherford, African-Americans noted, insisted on the most etiquette in "sensitive" areas like dining or lodging. He refused to eat with African-American men "lest it damage his work with southern men," and at one point suggested drawing a line down the middle of the dining room at Blue Ridge, the Y's training center, to divide the black and white diners (Moorland, no date; see also Chandler, 1994).

A narrow, apolitical belief in *efficiency* as a strategy for improvement underlay most social welfare programs for African-Americans, a concept related to the larger theory of assimilation. In assimilationists' thinking, peasants, whether from Europe or the South, could help the movement toward a more rational, modern, and racially tolerant society by "adjusting," that is, by rejecting their objectionable, country habits for behaviors that would facilitate their passage through "contact" toward "assimilation" in the race relations cycle (Park, 1926). On this basis, the Urban League in counseling job seekers urged upon them the "necessity for strict application to duties, punctuality, efficiency, proper deportment, and personal hygiene." "Rude" or "ridiculous" behavior by "greenhorns" dismayed many black social workers and Urban League offices published exhaustive lists of "dos and don'ts" for life both on the job and off. "DO NOT LOAF!" one list began. "Get a job at once. Do not live in crowded rooms. Do not carry on loud conversations in streetcars and public places. Do not think you can hold your job unless you are industrious, sober, and efficient" ("Sixteen Points," no date). The complex of efforts to improve workers' behavior was referred to as "uplift" and its proponents called by detractors the "uplift crowd." "Uplift" was not embraced by all social workers, but it was sufficiently widespread to be regularly, and often critically, commented upon within the black community. Opponents were not at all sure that cleanliness and hard work would bring reward in the North any more than they had in the South (see Litwack, 1991).

Liberal paternalism eschewed the language of rights in the provision of social services and talked instead of obligation and gratitude. Impoverished African-Americans were expected to approach benefactors hat-in-hand, grateful for both charity and advice. The bluesman with two-edged humor caught the posture well: "You gotta hanful of gimme, and a mouth full of much obliged" (quoted in Gabbin, 1985, p. 36). Booker T. Washington once explained gratitude to George Edmund Haynes, who was a fellow at the New York School of Philanthropy and later a leading social worker. Washington wrote Haynes in 1914 that an attitude was growing up around Fisk that "colored people should take charge of [the] University." "Now you and I both know," Washington instructed Haynes, "that this kind of agitation is most harmful and unwise. I am sure that the white people who during all these years have given of their money and of their time . . . have done so for the sole purpose of helping, and there is no set of people anywhere . . . more inclined to recognize colored people when the time comes when it can be done in a safe, helpful way. *The very worst thing that we could do is to indicate that we do not appreciate what has been done and is being done for us"* (Washington, 1984; emphasis added).

African-Americans who failed to acknowledge how "much obliged" they were for white assistance and instead asserted their right to services, were intimately familiar with the hostility and confusion such an attitude engendered. As one South Carolina white YMCA man angrily spluttered during the tense racial times that followed World War I, "The whites would be perfectly satisfied to do much for the Negro in the old terms and old ways if the Negro would be content with his status antebellum. We would build schools and so on, if they would only not *demand* and talk about citizenship" ("Minutes," no date).

African-American social service professionals considered the prescription that they be grateful and "only not *demand*" insulting to their intelligence and professional capabilities, and resisted this expectation vigorously. An example of such resistance to the prescription of gratitude comes from the letters of W. E. B. Du Bois. In 1925 Du Bois received a letter from a young student at the YMCA's Southern College. "Dear Sir:" the young man began, "I am preparing to make a study of the contribution of the YMCA to the negro race. The suggestion has been made to me by Dr. W. D. Weatherford that you in all likelihood possess much firsthand information which would be very valuable to me." Du Bois's (1973) reply to the student was characteristic and blunt:

My Dear Sir:

I have no information as to the contribution which the YMCA has made to the Negro race. I should imagine that the Negro race might teach the Southern College of the YMCA a good deal about Christianity.

Very sincerely yours,

W. E. B. Du Bois (1925)

At the same time that most of the white profession was pursuing a theory and practice of racial privilege and segregation, African-Americans, both working people and professionals, were being drawn into a maelstrom of economic, political, and theoretical activity that provided a far more effective challenge to poverty than did liberal paternalists' efforts to minister to a "weaker people." For the first time since the defeat of Reconstruction, hope based on some reality coursed through the black community, and it was migrants, soldiers, students, women, and professionals who provided the engine for change. The energy unleashed by the Great Migration transformed race relations in this country and thrust black Americans, black culture, and black political and economic life onto the international stage.

The entry of the United States into war in the spring of 1917 accelerated the changes dramatically. Overnight, the need for African-American soldiers and workers exploded; black citizens were mobilized to buy war bonds and black social service professionals enlisted to serve the troops. The movement of African-Americans was a highly conscious one, energized not only by individual economic need, but also by consciousness of the necessity to move quickly in this historical window of opportunity. Challenges to racial privilege abounded in the United States and among colonized people throughout the world. African-Americans organized the National Association for the Advancement of Colored People, the National Urban League, the United Negro Improvement Association, and the African Blood Brotherhood, and young people, determined to push beyond the limits a white supremacist society dictated, enrolled in colleges at six times their previous rate.

Dozen of black social service professionals worked with skill and uncommon energy in Urban Leagues, YMCAs, social agencies, and factories to place black migrants in jobs and "adjust" them to industry. In the early years of the Great Migration, when it seemed the whole race was participating in the effort to move blacks out of the terror and starvation of the South, Urban League secretaries worked passionately and with imagination to aid migrating families. Young and energetic, they answered letters demanding they "get busy for the South race," and could be found in nearly every train depot greeting the disembarking southerners (see Chandler 1996). In Pittsburgh, the Urban League received over two hundred letters from prospective migrants in the last two months of 1922, and after information about industrial opportunities was released in the black press, was flooded with fifteen hundred letters of inquiry (Clark, 1923). Keenly aware of the opportunities that these years offered the race, black professionals operated job registries, opened new areas of work for black men and women, helped organize bunkhouses and black company towns, pushed agencies to hire African-American social workers, and worked as welfare men and women in industry.

By 1915 the main work of the Urban League, the largest of the self-identified "black social work" organizations, was industrial. Migrant pressure and the near desperation of industrialists to finance programs that could move black workers into profit-rich wartime industry tended to push other social service work to the side. Forrester Washington, who was an early executive of the Detroit Urban League and in 1927 became the director of the Atlanta University School of Social Work, reported that in a one-year period the Detroit League placed 8,272 workers in jobs, 1,279 of whom were women. During 1919, the Chicago Urban League found jobs for more than 14,000 African-Americans, in each case keeping a careful record of their wages and conditions of work (Washington, no date).

Black industrial programs, at least for a brief time, had a passion and dynamic that distinguished them from other forms of welfare capitalism that emerged during this era of industrial expansion. In varying degrees, African-American professionals united in racial solidarity with black migrants and in so doing eased somewhat the suffocating paternalism that typified much of white welfare capitalism. The determination of migrants and professionals alike to improve the chances of the race gave an energy, breadth, and sense of social movement to placement and workplace services that has not since been duplicated. Eventually, the philosophy of "uplift" came to dominate many programs, and black social workers themselves were often caught, critics said, in a petit-bourgeois focus on individual advancement and loyal efficiency that served employers far better than workers ("Invisible World," 1920).

Uplifters tended to look through black workers, never seeing the rich-ness of their lives, the bitterness of their experience, nor their pride as working people. Jobs on the killing floors or in front of the great steel mill furnaces were dirty, noxious, heavy, and unhealthy. But still, factory posi-tions meant a step up in pay from domestic or janitorial work and release from those jobs' demeaning aspects. Workers could and did take pride in their ability to do the hardest work, and looked down on people "con-cerned with nothin' but a soft job." John B., a black worker at Carnegie Steel's Homestead plant, expressed a pride common among workers in heavy industry: "They gave me a job that nobody hardly wanted. . . . You had to handle the hot steel . . . and you had to handle it in your arms. Some of the boys they put on that job would walk off . . . [but] I stuck there. I stuck with it" (quoted in Gottlieb, 1987, p. 188). Black workers' justifiably felt successful, not only in holding down difficult jobs, but in the entire process of migration. The great promises had not been realized, but black newcomers were proud they had escaped the terror of the South, had established a base in industry, and had built communities in the North. Black men had found dignity in work and new skills and their wages, while unequal, were still significantly above those in the South. In the North, too, blacks had considerably more access to education, culture, and political and social organizations. It was what Sterling Brown celebrated in the poem *Strong Men*, "Ain't no hammah in dis lan', Strikes lak mine, bebby, Strikes lak mine" (1932).

At the same time, the industrial giants were successful, too, in relegat-ing blacks to the dirtiest and hottest jobs and creating a pool of semi- and unemployed workers that was largely defined by color. As segregation hardened, the relative position of blacks, in some minds, actually declined and complaints that there were no opportunities for advancement became insistent (Greer, 1985). African-American welfare workers in industry were tightly controlled, and industrial programs that were funded by industry increasingly served the employers' interests. It became apparent that securing jobs in industry, while critical to the advancement of the race, was only one step in the struggle for equality.

Finally, turning to the central theme of *The Professionalization of Poverty*, we can ask what was the relationship of these patterns of racial privilege in social services to social work's twentieth-century record sheet relative to poverty? In general, racial privilege and segregation effectively isolated most of the profession from the Great Migration and the other political, economic, and social movements that were transforming African-Ameri-can communities during the first part of the century. Most of white social work never saw the opportunity to address black poverty in the South that the Great Migration presented. As a result, white social work failed to benefit from the tremendous energy that the Great Migration unleashed, and retreated instead to practice that "adjusted" and segregated African-American workers and to narrow, undistinguished theories that were woefully inadequate to the political and economic challenges of the twentieth century. How much more powerful would have been a practice based on the strengths of African-American working people, one that included goals of racial unity, working-class organization, and equal social services for all. How much stronger would the profession's challenge to poverty have been if it had treasured the legacy of collective response to economic hardship in addition to the legacy of managing cases; encouraged instead of feared race pride; and lent its not-inconsiderable political position and moral weight to fighting instead of extending segregation. How weak in contrast was the analysis that put social service professionals workers in the position of lecturing workers on working hard and being efficient, as if these same workers weren't already pouring the steel, building the ships, cleaning the offices, and cutting the forests of the nation. "I am a Man who Beleave in right and Beleave in work and has worked all of my days and mean to work until I die," the migrant wrote (Scott, 1919, p. 296). Social work should have listened more carefully.

REFERENCES

"Average salaries for each department for the years 1922–1927." (no date [probably 1927]). Box B6, YMCA Archives. Social Welfare History Archives, University of Minnesota.

Brown, O. E. (1919). W. D. Weatherford's work as southern student secretary. *Intercollegian, 39*(December), 8–9.

Brown, S. (1932). Strong men. In *Southern Road*. New York: Harcourt Brace.

Chandler, S. (1994). Almost a partnership: African Americans, segregation, and the Young Men's Christian Association. *Journal of Sociology and Social Welfare,* 97–111.

Chandler, S. (1995). That biting, stinging thing which ever follows us: African-American social workers in World War I. *Social Service Review, 69,* 498–514.

Chandler, S. (1996). Industrial social work: African-American origins. *Journal of Progressive Human Services, 7,* 3–22.

Clark, J. T. (1923). "The migrant in Pittsburgh." *Opportunity 1*(October), 303–307.

Cooper, W. K. (1923). Letter to J. R. Mott, March 2. Box B6, YMCA Archives. Social Welfare History Archives, University of Minnesota.

Du Bois, W. E. B. (1914). The YMCA. *Crisis, 9*(2, December), 77, 81.

Du Bois, W. E. B. (1973). Letter to R. H. Ahearn, March 19, 1925. In H. Aptheker (Ed.), *The Correspondence of W. E. B. Du Bois, 1920–1929* (pp. 312–313). Millwood, NY: Kraus-Thomson Organization.

Duster, A. M. (Ed.) (1970). *Crusade for Justice: The Autobiography of Ida B. Wells.* Chicago: University of Chicago Press.

Frazier, E. F. (1957). *Black Bourgeoisie*. New York: MacMillan.

Gabbin, J. (1985). *Sterling A. Brown: Building the Black Aesthetic Tradition*. Westport, CT: Greenwood.

Gottlieb, P. (1987). *Making Their Own Way: Southern Blacks' Migration to Pittsburgh, 1916–1930*. Urbana: University of Illinois Press.

Greer, E. (1985). *Big Steel: Black Politics and Corporate Power in Gary, Indiana*. New York: Monthly Review.

Grossman, G. (1989). *Land of Hope: Chicago, Black Southerners, and the Great Migration*. Chicago: University of Chicago Press.

Hunton, A., & Johnson, K. (1920). *Two Colored Women with the American Expeditionary Force*. Brooklyn: Brooklyn Eagle. "The Invisible World of Negro Social Work" (1920). *Messenger*, 2(December), 174–177.

Litwack, L. (1991). Hellhound on my trail: Race relations in the south from reconstruction to the civil rights movement. In H. Knopke, R. Norrell, & R. Rogers (Eds.), *Opening Doors: Perspectives on Race Relations in Contemporary America* (pp. 3–25). Tuscaloosa: University of Alabama Press.

"Minutes of the Meeting of the Inter-Racial Commission" (no date [probably some time in the summer of 1919]). "Inter-Racial Commission." Box B7, YMCA Archives. Social Welfare History Archives, University of Minnesota.

Moorland, J. E. (no date [probably late 1915]). "Statement of important departmental facts for your strict confidential information." Box B3, YMCA Archives. Social Welfare History Archives, University of Minnesota.

Moton, R. R. (1923). Letter to J. R. Mott, March. Box B6, YMCA Archives. Social Welfare History Archives, University of Minnesota.

Park, R. (1926). Our racial frontiers on the Pacific. *Survey, 9*(May).

Peal, A. S. (1918). Letter to J. E. Moorland, March 12. Box B3, YMCA Archives. Social Welfare History Archives, University of Minnesota.

Philpott, T. (1978). *The Slum and the Ghetto: Neighborhood Deterioration and Middle Class Reform, Chicago, 1880–1930*. New York: Oxford University Press.

Scott, E. (Ed.) (1919). Additional letters of Negro migrants, 1916–1918. *Journal of Negro History* (October).

Shivery, L. D. (1936). The history of organized social work among Atlanta Negroes, 1890–1935. Unpublished masters thesis, Atlanta University. "Sixteen Points on How to Make Good" (no date [probably late 1910s]). Detroit Urban League papers. Michigan Historical Collections, Bentley Historical Library, University of Michigan.

Steward, G. (1927). Letter to E. F. Frazier, June 29. Correspondence, E. Franklin Frazier Papers. Moorland-Spingarn Research Center, Howard University.

Thomas, J. (1967). *My Story in Black and White*. New York: Exposition.

Washington, B. T. (1984). Letter to G. E. Haynes, 1914. In L. R. Harlan & R. Smock (Eds.), *The Booker T. Washington Papers* (Vol. 13, pp. 70–71). Chicago: University of Illinois Press.

Washington, B. T. (1914). A remarkable triple alliance: How a Jew is helping the Negro through the YMCA. *Outlook* (October 28).

Washington, F. (no date [probably late 1917]). The work in Detroit, Michigan. Detroit Urban League Papers. Carter G. Woodson Collection, Library of Congress.

Weatherford, W. D. (1911). *Negro Life in the South*. New York: Association.

Wilson, P. W. (1925). The projectile from the south. *Association Men* (October), 50–54.

Woodson, C. G. (1932). Comments on Negro education. *New York Age* (June 4), 10.

8

Harry Lawrence Lurie and Social Work's Questionable Commitment to Social and Economic Justice

JOE M. SCHRIVER

INTRODUCTION

The intent here is to continue to build upon a growing, more inclusive social work history by adding to the record the voice of Harry Lawrence Lurie (1892–1973), a Latvian immigrant who spent much of his professional life urging social workers to live up to our profession's commitment to achieving social and economic justice and eliminating poverty. As the twentieth century—also the first century of formal training and education for social work in the United States—comes to a close, it seems particularly important, indeed critical, that we reexamine and expand the scope of social work's historical record. Reexamination of social work's fundamental, if wavering, commitment to the elimination of poverty and the achievement of social and economic seems especially urgent today.

Throughout a professional life spanning the decades from the 1920s to the 1960s, Harry Lurie argued that the issues confronting social work were inextricably interwoven with conditions of poverty and social and economic injustice. During the twentieth century, social workers in the United States have often strayed from the profession's commitment to eradicating poverty and achieving social and economic justice. Many of us who call ourselves social workers seem confused about whether or not directly confronting poverty is even central to our mission. We seem to have even less consensus about the nature of our responsibilities as members of a profession claiming a mission so profound as the achievement of social and economic justice.

Do virtually all of the pressing issues of concern to social workers—oppression, inequality, racism, sexism, teen pregnancy, health care, immigration, welfare reform, aging, child welfare, violence, and a host of others—have as common denominators the eradication of poverty and the attainment of social and economic injustice? For Harry Lurie, the answer to this fundamental question, was a most decided—yes.

LURIE'S EARLY YEARS AND INFLUENCE

Harry Lawrence Lurie came to the United States as a six-year-old immigrant from Latvia in 1898. His father and his older sister had preceded him and the rest of his family in the move to the United States because "it was the rare family that could finance the trip for all at the same time" (Robert L. Aronson, personal communication to author, April 4, 1984). According to Lurie's daughter, Alison, "[M]y father's family left Latvia for America for a combination of economic and political reasons, hoping to exchange poverty and persecution for opportunity and freedom and equality, like so many other immigrants of the time" (Schriver 1987b, p. 515). Harry Lurie's experiences of the dire consequences of social, political and economic injustice, persecution, and poverty, at a very early age, helped set the stage for his lifelong passion, expressed through his social work career, for achieving social and economic justice.

As the feminist movement many years later was to attest, the personal was indeed political, and Harry Lurie was among those early few in social work who pointed to this inseparable connection. He entered the world of professional social work in the 1920s having been heavily influenced by the profession's Progressive era forebears: "[T]hese were the days of the initial steps in industrial and civic improvement, in the development of labor standards and safeguards against epidemics, accidents, and excessive exploitation of labor" (Lurie 1961, p. 62). The progressive heritage included the conviction "that poverty could be eliminated in the growing productivity of a prosperous country" (ibid., p. 86).

The influences of the Progressive era were felt at the university level as well, in the interest in studying and addressing social problems. It was in this context of optimism in the late Progressive era that Lurie completed his graduate education in the emerging field of sociology at the University of Michigan.

The term "sociology" was accepted as the designation for this new approach to the study of the problems of society. . . . With the work of Charles H. Cooley, Franklin Giddings in sociology, and Simon Patton and John R. Commons in economics, a theoretical basis was being established for the efforts of social workers and reformers whose programs of social action were being considered as "applied sociology." (Lurie, 1960, p. 31)

Bruno (1957, p. 134) called this period "the honeymoon state of the interrelationship between theory and practice; between the teaching of sociology and the practice of social work." Trattner noted later, however, that the honeymoon was a short one:

> [S]ociologists felt a need to disassociate themselves and their research from social workers who, they felt, were too value-oriented and thus not objective enough, while social workers felt that sociology was too theoretical and not practical enough. (1974, p. 168)

Lurie did not seem to reflect this binary approach to the two disciplines. For example, he noted the possible contributions of social work to sociology: "The experiences of the social worker may effect marked changes in social theory. . . . It has been said, with justification, that the well trained social worker is potentially the sociologist of the future" (Lurie 1927, p. 202).

In his rise to prominence in the new profession of social work in the 1920s and through the 1930s and 1940s, Lurie remained true to the basic tenets of the Progressive years. He was often, in the coming years, to expand on the ideas and beliefs that caught hold during the Progressive years and was to call upon the profession to remain true to and nurture its Progressive era heritage.

In 1925, Lurie accepted a position as superintendent of the Jewish Social Service Bureau of Chicago. It was while he was in this position that he also became associated with the University of Chicago School of Social Service Administration as a faculty member. Lurie integrated his beliefs about social and economic issues with the emerging areas of professional social work practice and education during his association with the Chicago School and its principals, Edith Abbott and Sophonisba Breckenridge. Lurie later credited Abbott and Breckenridge with being most responsible for his approach to professional social work (Lurie, 1961, p. vii).

Lurie entered the social work education arena at a time of considerable tumult about what exactly should be the focus of education for the emerging profession. Should social work education be technical and individually focused or should it be broad and more concerned with the social causes of poverty and distress? The Chicago school, with which Lurie was newly connected, differed markedly from many of its eastern counterparts on the answer to this question. Lubove notes, for example:

> The Chicago School of Civics and Philanthropy, although not immune from the pressures toward specialization, practicality, and casework, exhibited a distinctive interest in social research, public welfare administration, and a broad professional education. (Lubove, 1965, pp. 143–144)

However, the Chicago approach would at most provide a challenge to social work that was not fully or readily accepted by many in social work circles. The development of social work was instead to shift course dramatically in the 1920s, away from broad, scientific approaches to the impersonal and social causes of poverty and distress. The shift would lead social work to an overriding concern for individual failure and maladjustment as the factors most needing attention by social workers if people's problems were to be ameliorated.

The advocacy by Abbott and Breckenridge (and later Abbott's sister Grace) for broad, scientific, university-based social work education significantly influenced Lurie's perspectives on the proper focus of professional social work practice and education. That Lurie proselytized the broad view of social work education is evident in a speech he gave in early 1931, in which he stressed the "solid gains" that social work had made in its early Progressive years. Among these gains could be counted the "social and economic studies, surveys, causes" and an "emphasis upon professional education," which did not produce "'trained workers' in the sense of trained monkeys" but was instead "education to see the whole perspective of social problems from a historical viewpoint and in the light of modern social knowledge" (Lurie, 1931d).

Lurie remained a forceful advocate of social reform and called repeatedly for social work to reverse its emphasis on casework and return to an overriding or at least an equal emphasis on the role of impersonal social and economic factors in the problems people faced. In 1927 Lurie reminded social workers of the "dual aspect of the family caseworking agency":

> The social motive of family agencies—their desire to achieve social ends or improvements—has resulted in an active interest in matters of social policies, social and economic institutions, and social legislation. (Lurie, 1927, pp. 203–204)

Nevertheless in 1928 Lurie concluded, "It might be said that the social worker is emphasizing at the present time the importance of psychological factors" (Lurie, 1928b, p. 580). He was not, however, willing to concede that psychological factors were the only concerns of the caseworker. It was his contention, rather, that both "the social and the psychological factors demand intelligent attention" (Lurie, 1928b, p. 581)

In the late 1920s Lurie challenged both the overwhelming acceptance by social workers of an individual-psychological definition of problems requiring individual adjustment rather than social change and the larger view in the U.S. social environment of the 1920s that, because of apparent economic prosperity in the country, social reform was unnecessary. Lurie noted, for example, in 1928 that a study conducted by the University of

Chicago and the Chicago Council of Social Agencies found that there were large numbers of persons living below the currently accepted minimum standard of living who were not being aided by standard casework services or by relief policy "based upon destitution." Because of this he called for "the organized community [to] find other methods of aiding such families during times of crises and of assuring to them a continuous, uninterrupted income which would make possible a satisfactory standard of living" (Lurie, 1928a, pp. 292–293; Schriver, 1987b, p. 518).

Some of the specific measures for remedying these situations of economic need resulting from the shortcomings of the larger socioeconomic system prefigured demands Lurie would make during the Great Depression. He suggested as possible remedies, for example, "general wage increases, which, considering the tremendous productive capacity of this country, seems an attainable goal . . . [or] family allowances and family subsidies added to a basic wage policy" (Lurie, 1928a, p. 291; Schriver, 1987b, p. 518).

Central to Lurie's argument for such possibilities was a theme he would repeat many times in the future, "[T]he highly developed industrial and economic organization of this country can produce a standard of living for all greater than the inadequate minimum now afforded to large sections of the population" (Lurie, 1928a, p. 293; Schriver, 1987b, p. 518).

At the end of the 1920s Harry Lurie had solidified his position concerning social work practice and education as that of "cause" rather than "function," to use Porter Lee's often cited 1929 differentiation of the dual concerns of social work (Schriver, 1987b, p. 518).

COMING OF AGE IN THE GREAT DEPRESSION

At the onset of the Great Depression, in addition to aligning himself with "cause" in social work, Lurie had also achieved a place of respect and prominence within the social work mainstream. He had become a respected and sought-after teacher of social work. He had become the director of a major private Jewish family service agency in Chicago. He had been appointed by the governor of Illinois to the State Board of Public Welfare Commissioners. He was active in the American Association of Social Workers (AASW), the mainstream professional organization of social workers. Jacob Fisher, who both worked for and with Lurie in several capacities over a long period of time, provides a helpful thumbnail sketch of the mature Lurie. Harry Lurie, according to Fisher (1980):

> possessed what one social-work journal described as a corrosive intellect. He had indeed a mind which saw through the conventional pieties on public issues, social and economic. . . . Now and then you caught a saturnine look

on his wide expressive mouth, as though he was amused at the sluggish
thinking of those he had to deal with, but he was essentially a modest person, diffident in manner, uninterested in promoting a cause or following.
Nevertheless, by sheer intellectual acuity he usually dominated committees
of which he was a member, and he was often requested to prepare their
reports, since he was adept at articulating and resolving conflicting points of
view and was a master in the preparation of a carefully thought-through,
integrated analysis of the subject assigned to the committee. (pp. 68–69)

In 1930, at the onset of the Great Depression, Lurie moved from Chicago
to accept the position of executive director of the Bureau of Jewish Social
Research in New York City. The bureau later expanded to become the
Council of Jewish Federations and Welfare Funds. The council was a
national fund-raising, planning, and research organization for Jewish
Social Welfare efforts in the United States, somewhat analogous to United
Way of America. Lurie served as executive director of the council until his
retirement in the 1950s.

The depression experience confirmed and gave new voice to Lurie's
long-held position regarding the responsibilities of social work beyond
that of mere casework. During the depression years he became intensely
involved in trying to secure public and specifically federal responsibility
for the needy masses. In order to begin to meet the needs of the destitute
more adequately, Lurie called repeatedly for the assumption and rapid
expansion of governmental responsibility for relief services. His notions of
this responsibility went far beyond the traditional and insufficient local
poor relief to an assumption of major responsibility by the federal government. He was convinced that any significant effort to remedy the depression crisis must include an expanded and effective program of public
social services by the federal government.

After the depression hit with full force in the latter part of 1929 and continued unabated through 1930 and 1931, Lurie became increasingly
adamant about the collective responsibility of the community for coming
to the aid of its neediest members. This, he argued, could only be accomplished through organized and far-reaching public social welfare measures in concert with, but not competing with private social welfare
services.

In a paper published in the 1931 *Proceedings of the National Conference of
Social Work,* Lurie targeted social workers' responsibility for foot dragging
in accepting and pushing for increased governmental responsibility for
social welfare measures (Lurie, 1931b):

If we previously believed that poverty or economic insecurity of the individual was largely a condition of personal maladjustment best served by the
case work method, preferably exercised by private benevolence, the exigen-

cies of the present period of Depression have radically altered our assumptions. . . . We have too long been dominated in case work by an economic philosophy remote from the actualities of our highly complicated industrial and economic organization. (p. 212)

Lurie urged social workers to critically examine the implications of their almost total adherence to an individualistic economic philosophy:

It was accepted as a cardinal principle of social work that the problem of poverty was not the direct concern of the entire community but only those who desired to be charitable. This was corollary to the belief that poverty was an indication of incompetence if not of personal abnormality. (ibid., pp. 212–226)

Though Lurie may have realized the need for more fundamental means of dealing with the inherent irregularities of the economic system, others in social work had not yet become convinced by depression conditions of the need for fundamental changes in the status quo. Even that paragon of progressivism, Hull House, in 1932 originally sided with Hoover rather than Roosevelt's platform for the New Deal, believing that depression problems would be naturally remedied when business recovered (Lurie, 1935a, p. 18).

To Lurie there was really only one major reason for not resolving the "basic problem of our social order:"

Although political leaders are frequently not as candid as they might well be, the opposition to federal aid will be intrinsically the reluctance to tax wealth for the benefit of the poor, no matter what other valid or specious reasons may be openly advanced. (Lurie, 1931c, p. 538)

LURIE AND THE SOCIAL WORK MAINSTREAM: AASW AND MENTAL HYGIENE

During the depression years, the American Association of Social Workers (AASW), the mainstream organization representing professional social work, did shift more of its energy to concerns about unemployment and poverty. Lurie chaired a Subcommittee on Unemployment of the AASW Commission on Unemployment. In that capacity he prepared and presented a statement on unemployment relief at the May 1932 joint session of the AASW and the Professional Standards and Education Division of the NCSW. He had presented this same statement only one week earlier at a hearing of the United States Senate Committee on Manufactures. The statement was "a summary of the status of unemployment relief based upon current information received from social workers in touch with conditions in their own communities" (Lurie, 1932, p. 223). The report reflected the "intellectual acuity" of Lurie to which Fisher (1980) referred.

The report included information "received within the last two weeks" from twenty-nine cities in sixteen states across the country. The picture that emerged was one "of distress growing daily more desperate." Funds for relief were being diverted away from other essential social services; entire twelve month budgets for unemployment relief were being depleted in only three or four months. Exhaustion of public funds in New York, for example, was resulting in a "radical and serious curtailment in the public school program." In Cleveland some hospitals were threatened with shutdown. Generally, "communities are meeting the problem only by a continuous process of spreading their relief thin" (Lurie, 1932, p. 223).

The situation was so desperate in some places that agencies were simply abandoning their efforts to provide relief entirely or to entire groups in need. This was especially true in the South and Southwest and was particularly the case for services to African-Americans and Mexican-Americans. In Houston, for example, Lurie pointed out that "applications are not taken from unemployed Mexican or colored families. They are being asked to shift for themselves." This troubling information provides striking evidence of discrimination against persons of color being practiced by relief agencies (Lurie, 1932, p. 223). It also provides a dramatic example of why African-American families and communities needed such adaptive strategies as mutual aid, self-help, and empowerment efforts with their "pennies, nickels and dimes" to survive during these years (Burwell, 1995).

Lurie also worked with AASW to make recommendations for a national "program of social security" as chair of its Subcommittee on Future Coordination of a Federal Dependency Relief Program. According to the committee's report, the program should include federal responsibility, it should be "country-wide," it should receive sufficient financial support to "allow for long-term planning," and it should include the concept of prevention (Subcommittee on Future Coordination of Federal Dependency Relief Program, 1934, p. 1).

At the same time Lurie was calling upon the public, through government, to reverse what he considered its archaic and destructive notions about the exclusively individual responsibility for need, he called upon social workers to do likewise. In an address he delivered to the New York City Conference of Social Work in May 1931, he chided social workers for their general lack of preparedness for the crisis of the depression. He argued that:

> social work cannot consider itself a useful adjunct of the economic system only during periods of prosperity. . . . It has a continuing responsibility for

problems growing out of the economic depression as well as those which are matters of social concern during more normal times. (Lurie, 1931a)

Specifically, he said,

The primary need in social work theory is the realization that the economic system within which we function is subject not alone to occasional dislocations, such as that of the present depression, but that there are gross inadequacies and inequalities involved in the creation of social problems with which we are concerned during more normal periods. (Lurie, 1931a)

In a presentation at a conference in New York in late 1932 that received coverage both in the *New York Times* and early in 1933 in *Survey,* a popular journal dealing with social issues and widely read by social workers, Lurie noted some optimism that social workers were perhaps beginning to realize the need for more comprehensive approaches than mere casework. This optimism was most likely increased by the election of FDR. Lurie noted, for example:

We are beginning to realize now in social case work that we have overemphasized personal factors and influences and have disregarded or have been little concerned with the equally important impersonal factors and impersonal relationships of the individual to the social and economic order. ("Public Aid Asked," 1932; Lurie, 1933b; Schriver, 1987b, pp. 523)

He concluded that "the future of social work lies more in organization of social forces than in the methods of casework. . . . Casework . . . is usually a poor substitute for inadequate income and is not a genuine solution for the problems of poverty" (Lurie, 1933b, p. 61; Schriver, 1987b, p. 524). Social workers must realize instead that "there are many personal problems which can be solved by adequate opportunity." Social workers must

relinquish the idea that case work in itself is the key to the solution of major social problems. The case worker must become more of a social worker intent upon the solution of social problems and less of a technician skilled in methods of adapting individuals to the status quo. (Lurie, 1933b, pp. 61–64; Schriver, 1987b, p. 524)

Lurie was not entirely alone. Paul Kellog, another prominent social worker of the day, put it more succinctly: "You cannot deal effectively with an inferiority complex on an empty stomach" (Trattner, 1974, p. 243).

One of the counterforces to the shift by some social workers toward concerns for addressing poverty particularly troubling to Lurie was Mental Hygiene Theory. Mental Hygiene Theory was espoused by an increasing number of social workers in the 1930s, including such prominent mainstream leaders as Helen Hall. In a 1933 response to a paper Hall had written titled, "Current American Methods of Handling Unemployment in the Light of Present Mental Hygiene Knowledge," Lurie referred to the paper as evidence "that our unemployment programs have definitely reflected . . . the more orthodox doctrines." He was, of course referring to such current theories as Mental Hygiene, which placed the responsibility for dealing with unemployment squarely on the individual's shoulders (Lurie, 1933c; Schriver, 1987b).

Lurie highlighted his concerns by quoting a popular pamphlet read by many administrators and social workers of the time called "Morale—The Mental Hygiene of Unemployment." The pamphlet had been issued by the National Committee for Mental Hygiene (Lurie, 1933c, p. 1; Schriver, 1987b, pp. 524–525). Some of the suggestions in the pamphlet would have been laughable had they not been offered so seriously. According to the pamphlet, the social worker's role was that of raising the morale of the unemployed. The job of "fundamental social reconstruction" should be left to others. Good mental hygiene included "work for health's sake." Diversions such as choral singing and folk dancing, according to the pamphlet, were recommended for dealing with the problems of unemployment because

> a vigorous draining-off or even an explosion of nervous energy . . . seems to be essential for thoroughly normal living . . . but when one is deprived of the opportunity to find legitimate release for accumulations of nervous energy through one's job, then wise social workers and the wise community in general will provide other outlets. (Lurie, 1933c, pp. 2–3; Schriver, 1987b, p. 525)

Such "outlets" might consist of "hobbies and organized recreation, blowing off steam through soap box oratory should also be permitted to drain off unwholesome feelings and attitudes." Lurie also described what he called "various types of modern evangelism" put forth in the pamphlet and their false logic. He quoted an excerpt from the pamphlet:

> In the first place hardship and suffering alone do not create poor mental health, nor do these things alone lower morale. What usually does cause mental ill-health and lessened morale is a lack of personal inner resources to help people stand (or adjust to) hardships or suffering. These resources may be normal dependence on religion, patriotism, on personal ambition, . . . and many other things. (Lurie, 1933c, pp. 2–4; Schriver, 1987b, p. 525)

Lurie went on to note:

> After outlining ways in which hardships and discomforts may compensate and even become pleasurable it is suggested that men and women "are buoyed up to suffering hardship in the present world by the belief that such

suffering is a prerequisite for happiness in the world to come." (Lurie, 1933c, pp. 3–4; Schriver, 1987b, p. 525)

Such a countervailing force to a social work theory grounded in social and economic justice as that of Mental Hygiene Theory brings into bold relief the contradictions in the profession of such concern to Lurie.

LURIE AND THE NEW DEAL

Lurie followed closely and commented often on the unfolding of Roosevelt's New Deal efforts. Initially Lurie saw great hope that New Deal programs might permanently and from fundamentally different philosophical premises address the critical concerns of unemployment and poverty. His optimism about realizing this potential was to shift significantly as the depression and New Deal continued. In a letter to Harry Hopkins, also a social worker, Lurie expressed his sense of optimism about the "Federal Civil Work Plan:"

> I consider it an enlightened and revolutionary departure form the antiquated theories of poor relief. . . . [I]t will set a precedent in this country for all future planning with reference to social responsibility. . . . What I like particularly are the aspects which make joblessness rather than destitution the basis for the service rendered, that it maintains high standards of wages thus throwing overboard the pernicious theory of "less eligibility" for people without jobs. (Lurie, 1933d)

Lurie believed this to be especially the case "if it can be made a permanent policy" (Lurie,p. 1933d). In Lurie's opinion, the Roosevelt program marked "a constructive advance in the history of public welfare in the United States." The unemployed worker was no longer seen as "an instance of individual pathological maladjustment but as a jobless worker for whom the nation has an obligation to provide normal remunerative employment" (Lurie, 1933a, pp. 1–2) and for whom "distress is not due to their own shortcoming but to a breakdown of the social and economic machinery." New Deal programs were especially important to these people and "partial or even temporary failure" of the New Deal programs they depended on would cause so much "disappointment and disillusion" that there could be no guarantee they would "follow socially useful or constructive leadership" (Lurie, 1933e, p. 1).

However, Lurie's hopes for permanency were soon dashed:

> In March 1934 Hopkins abruptly terminated the CWA job program. It was a disquieting turn of events for social workers, accustomed after twelve

months of the new administration to glad tidings only in the news from Washington. (Fisher, 1980, p. 52)

It was Lurie's assessment that those opposing the program embodied "the discredited do-nothing-to-interfere-with-private-business theory and the deluded hope that business recovery will take place more rapidly if we neglect the unemployed and leave them to endure suffering and privation" (Lurie, 1934).

LURIE, SOCIAL WORK'S LEFT WING, AND THE MAINSTREAM

Even during the early, more robust New Deal days, a number of social workers, perhaps most prominently Mary Van Kleeck, called for much stronger measures. Van Kleeck was director of the Division of Industrial Studies of the Russell Sage Foundation. At a 1933 AASW-sponsored Conference on National Economic Objectives, she gave a luncheon presentation called "A Planned Economy." In it she suggested that any national economic objective should be analyzed in terms of whether it was:

being advocated as a means to patch up the present situation, save the status quo, postpone a little longer any more searching look into our economic scheme of things, or is it being advocated as one step further toward socialized industry. ("Transcript of the Luncheon Meeting," 1933, p. 5)

A lively discussion among those attending the luncheon followed Van Kleeck's presentation. It was facilitated by Lurie. John Fitch, a member of the faculty of the New York School of Social Work, now Columbia University School of Social Work, took a decidedly conservative stand. He contended: "We can't get a controlled economy in this country without a complete change in our governmental machinery, not merely a change in the capitalist system but a complete change in the political set-up . . . either by amending the constitution in the usual way, that slow process, or by revolution." Another attendee took a more pragmatic stance: "All of us who have any social vision at all realize we are shock absorbers or stop-traps or palliatives in a decaying system" ("Transcript of the Luncheon Meeting," 1933, p. 34).

Lurie also increasingly presented critical and radical appraisals of the leadership and direction for social work. He argued that "much of social work theory and training is meaningless, inexact, untrue and if adhered to in part anti-social" (Lurie, 1935b). To remedy this, social workers needed "economic and political intelligence," areas in which social workers were "practically illiterate." Lurie also called repeatedly for a close alliance between social work and labor, even though antiradicalism, racial prejudice, intense competition, and a powerful status quo were presenting major obstacles to the labor movement itself (Lurie, 1935b).

Lurie was convinced the potential for moving social work toward such an alliance with labor and toward organized political opposition to the status quo lay in what he termed the "new leadership in social work, crude or dogmatic or inexperienced as it may be." This new leadership came to be known as the rank-and-file movement (Lurie, 1935b). For the profession generally, according to Fisher, the rank-and-file movement represented "the return to social work . . . of the concern with larger social issues characteristic of the social work of the progressive era in American politics" (Fisher, 1980, p. 5).

The relationship of the movement and the mainstream AASW was rocky at best. Rank-and-filers viewed AASW as an elitist organization responding primarily to the few mainstream status quo types who controlled it. Harry Lurie often acted as a bridge between the rank-and-file movement and the social work mainstream in AASW. Lurie supported and actively participated in many of the activities of the movement throughout its relatively short life. He was a frequent contributor of articles to *Social Work Today,* the journal of the movement. He served as a contributing editor to the journal in its early days and participated in the movement- organized social workers' discussion clubs, the movement's first national conference, and its ongoing efforts to support unionization.

A fundamental barrier to a more activist stance, such as that reflected in the rank-and-file movement, was what Lurie believed to be most social workers' refusal to admit the essentially conservative nature of casework. In an article appearing in *Social Work Today,* Lurie described the dilemma confronting the caseworker. The dilemma for these workers was whether to "continue to create little islands of security," which might give some tangible results, or to "plunge into the general turmoil and engage in the larger battle for social welfare." Lurie believed that "the little islands of security which case workers are attempting to create within the general oceans of insecurity are weak and unsubstantial and at the mercy of the first storm that blows" (Lurie, 1935c, pp. 13–15; Schriver, 1987b, pp. 526–527).

His preference was clearly

> to keep social workers primarily concerned with social problems and with social and economic institutions. . . . Since so large a part of the distress and maladjustment confronting individuals grows out of social rather than individual limitations. (Lurie, 1938, p. 9; Schriver, 1987b, p. 529)

Even in the mainstream Lurie found some allies for his position. For example, Dorothy Wysor Smith, executive secretary of the Travelers Aid Society of Los Angeles, in response to a lecture Lurie gave in Los Angeles wrote him to share her sense of camaraderie: "Sometime I have felt that my eastern colleagues must somehow all have gone 'batty'—or that I have myself—because of the amount of jargon and 'deep therapy' patter which seems to emanate from leaders in the east" (Smith, 1937).

However, more commonly, rather than finding allies among the mainstream, Lurie was faced with considerable differences of opinion between his views and those of mainstream stalwarts. This was certainly reflected in his response to Helen Hall's espousal of mental hygiene as an approach to dealing with unemployment described earlier. In addition, the conservative stance of the New York School of Social Work's John Fitch to a planned economy discussed above was not atypical of Lurie's mainstream colleagues.

Particularly illustrative of these substantive differences of opinion is Lurie's 1931 review of a new text, *A Changing Psychology in Social Case Work*, by Virginia Robinson. Equally informative are some of the responses to Lurie's review. Of Robinson's perspective, Lubove (1965, pp. 113–114) has noted, "In Miss Robinson's estimation, social work came of age in the 1920's, when interest shifted from the environment to the meaning of experience within the individual psyche." In his review Lurie sternly challenged this perspective. Instead of social work coming of age in the 1920s as reflected by the perspective in Robinson's book, Lurie considered the book to be "the literary culmination of the period from which we have emerged" (1931e, p. 488). Specifically, he suggested

> With this newer and perhaps more socially significant concern [the depression], the last decade of development in case work begins to take on the characteristics of a historical period heavily littered with partially assimilated knowledge and pseudo scientific theories. The fog of psychoanalytic terminology may be mystifying to the uninitiated but it has apparently been pregnant with profound meaning to the enthusiasts. . . . Evaluating *A Changing Psychology in Social Case Work* is undoubtedly more difficult on account of our present detachment from the problems which concern the author. (ibid.)

Lurie found particularly untenable Robinson's limitation of the focus of the casework relationship to that between the worker and the client and her insistence that the relationship be used "on deeper and deeper levels to release his [sic] conflicts, to project his impulses, to work through his problems, and define himself as a real self in differentiation from the other." Lurie's response was, "The present period in social work with its more realistic concern will undoubtedly operate to restore a sane balance in casework theory. The 'other' it might be suggested is perhaps the whole social and economic environment . . . and not the personification of the mother 'object'" (ibid.). Robinson's rejoinder was to wonder "how the social case worker can enter into this relationship between the client and his [*sic*] social economic environment. On this point we could probably differ forever" (Robinson, 1931).

Lurie's review also sparked some mainstream support that reflected the kind of changes a few in the mainstream were trying to make in their own approaches to practice. Joanna Colcord, a prominent mainstream social worker and director of the Charity Organization Department of the Russell Sage Foundation, wrote Lurie and suggested that he "should have a public vote of thanks" for questioning Robinson's approach. She noted also in the letter that the depression had "completely changed the focus of her duties" (Colcord, 1931).

In contrast to Lurie's negative review, Bertha Capen Reynolds, one of the forebears of psychiatric casework, wrote a very positive review of Robinson's book for *The Family*. Shortly after her review, she received a letter from Florence Sytz of the Tulane University School of Social Work. Sytz argued, "The time has not yet come when social workers can confine their interest and activity to the realm of emotional adjustment, either for themselves or for their client." In her autobiography, Reynolds observed of Sytz's comments, "Would that this warning had been heeded in the years to follow" (Reynolds, 1963, pp. 121–122). Reynolds eventually changed her perspective to include a clearly Marxist conceptualization of society. In addition, she was to be associated with Lurie in a number of his activities with the rank-and-file movement, including serving as a contributing editor with him for the rank-and-filers' journal, *Social Work Today*.

Both the opposition and the alliances reflected in the responses to Robinson's book and to the reviews of both Lurie and Reynolds suggest a mainstream in the early 1930s in somewhat of a vortex. On the one hand were the mainstream advocates for continuing on the psychological/internal path set in the 1920s such as Robinson, Hall, and Fitch. On the other hand were mainstream leaders such as Colcord and Reynolds, who significantly altered their perspectives and their practice to become centered more on social and economic environmental factors.

As the depression faded into the World War II years, Lurie's activities and concerns became more focused on the international arena. Clearly to Lurie, however, the international scene and the domestic front were closely interrelated. In 1939, Lurie joined John Boland and Eduard Lindeman, both prominent social work figures, in calling for tolerance and respect for diversity in the face of growing hostility toward immigrants in the United States. They argued that "[Humanity] will grow into wisdom of an age in which [it] will understand that [its] diversity is not [its] problem, but [its] resource in social and cultural development" (Boland, Lindeman, & Lurie, 1939, p. 3). This call for acceptance and tolerance must have had a special urgency for Lurie, whose own roots were those of a Jewish immigrant.

A CAREER WINDS DOWN: A PERIOD OF
REFLECTION AND GUIDANCE

During the later 1940s and into the 1950s Lurie increasingly reflected on the state of social work education and practice in his writing and speeches. In 1946 he was asked to speak about "The Next Twenty-Five Years" of social work. He recounted the continuing development of social work and noted: "Social work has become an acknowledged occupation as well as a profession beginning to define and adhere to its standards" (Lurie, 1946, pp. 1–2). Lurie also addressed the current situation in social work in the speech. He noted with concern the changes that were occurring in the staffing of social welfare programs. He pointed specifically to the fact that many of the new social work–related positions were being filled by persons without "professional training and experience." He believed

> it is significant that so many of the fields of social welfare which grew out of the matrix of social work are administered by persons recruited from fields other than social work. The statistics have not been assembled but it is obvious that economists, administrators and executives, psychiatrists and other types of professions now have major responsibility for some of these activities. (Lurie, 1946, p. 3)

He suggested the reason for this trend was not the limited supply of available professional social workers, but the deficiencies in the education of social workers:

> We may well raise the question—whether in training and experience, the graduates of our Schools of Social Work are well equipped for these administrative positions as are the business executives, the economists, the general administrators, the politicians who are selected instead? (ibid., p. 3)

He used the occasion to review the present state of education:

> We are supposed to have a basic grounding in our undergraduate days in the social sciences . . . in sociology, in economics, in psychology and psychiatry. . . . It should lay the groundwork for an understanding of personality, of personal and group relationships and of the basic problems of community life. When we attend schools of social work . . . supposedly this knowledge is to be deepened and we are to learn special techniques required in social case work, public welfare, group work, social agency administration and community organization. (Lurie, 1946)

Given this broad preparation, Lurie wondered why so many social workers still chose "the limited areas of our techniques in dealing with individual maladjustment" rather than the broader areas of concern such as "economic, social and political organization" (Lurie, 1946, pp. 4–6; Schriver, 1987a, pp. 123–124).

Lurie's position had not changed regarding the importance of social workers' involvement in social reform nor had his position regarding social workers' continuing ventures "into the fields of psychiatry and psychoanalysis":

> I am firmly convinced, however, that we can make a better contribution if we set as our goal that we are primarily concerned with becoming first rate social workers along the broadest possible lines rather than be satisfied with becoming second or third rate psycho-analysts. (Lurie, 1946, p. 6)

In his later years, Lurie also continued to stress the role of social work as "a series of challenges to the existing order" (Lurie, 1949). After his retirement in 1954 Lurie continued to work to increase the emphasis on social and economic justice in social work's "underlying philosophy." One area in which he played a key role in this philosophical expansion was through the development of community organization as an accepted method of professional social work practice. Lurie was the project consultant for the community organization component of the CSWE-sponsored curriculum study edited by Werner Boehm and published in 1959. It was not until 1962 that Community Organization was formally accepted by the CSWE as a major and recognized area of social work education and practice along with groupwork and work with individuals. In some respects this change represented an institutionalization within social work of the social action/social reform function, which had been at the heart of so much of Lurie's professional life. He believed

> the development of the teaching of community organization in schools of social work potentially offers one of the most valuable and effective vehicles for developing basic values and standards for the broad field of welfare services both under governmental and voluntary auspices. (Boehm, 1959, p. 58.)

CONCLUSION

The uncertain reception by his contemporaries of his stand for a pivotal place in the social work canon for addressing poverty and social and economic injustice seems eerily familiar in the late 1990s. Many of the issues Lurie found intertwined with poverty and social and economic justice—discrimination, immigration induced by poverty and persecution, international issues, unemployment—are still with us today. As was the case in Lurie's day, social workers are uncertain and timid about the roles they should play. As in Lurie's day, the lure of internal approaches through psychotherapy primarily for the benefits of a privileged, often white middle class, offer irresistible attraction to many social workers.

As in Lurie's day, our professional organizations seem as uncertain as their individual members about effective roles and strategies for addressing poverty and social and economic injustice. As was Lurie's concern, our hunger for respectability through professionalization and our fears of being unpopular because we dare to challenge the social, economic, and political status quo seem too often to have undermined our vision and direction as a profession. Lurie's perspective seems especially important at the close of the twentieth century when the belief in collective responsibility for those unable to attain the necessary resources for a decent and secure standard of living seems daily to be eroding at the hands of those who would return the pendulum to an extreme version of "rugged individualism."

Perhaps renewed strength can be found in the example set by Harry Lurie's conviction that the world and the social worker's responsibilities within it need not be viewed as either/or, but must be viewed as both/and. There is room for both a social and economic justice cause–focus and an individual-based function–focus in social work, he claimed. His challenge to social work was (and is as relevant today as during his times) to embrace both these functions at least equally. His preference, no doubt, was that the social and economic justice function be given primacy and be used to guide all of our work with individuals. On reflection at the end of the twentieth century we are hard pressed for evidence that we have found a balance between the individual and the social emphases in our profession.

We might end this chapter by wondering why Lurie's call for a profession concerned simultaneously with critical analysis and responsive action at both social and individual levels did not prevail. Why have we been unable to strike that essential, but elusive balance necessary to build a practice founded equally on understanding the complexities of individual human behavior and those of the social environment? Is it possible that we have been unable to do so because we have not yet learned that the personal really is political and that—at the level of the profession—we must be able to engage in both self- and collective analysis in order to change ourselves, our profession, and the world?

REFERENCES

Boehm, Werner (Ed.) (1959). *Curriculum Study,* Vol. 4, Harry L. Lurie, *The Community Organization Method in Social Work Education.* New York: Council on Social Work Education.

Boland, John, Lindeman, Eduard, & Lurie, Harry L. (1939). Upon this we are built *Social Work Today, 7*, 3.

Bruno, Frank, J. (1957). *Trends in Social Work, 1874–1956*. New York: Columbia University Press.

Burwell, Yolanda (1995). Shifting the historical lens: Early economic empowerment among African-Americans. *Journal of Baccalaureate Social Work, 1*(1), 25–37.

Colcord, Joanna (1931). Letter to Lurie, October 2. Lurie Papers, Box 2, Folder 26, University of Minnesota, National Social Welfare Archives Center.

Fisher, Jacob (1980). *The Response of Social Work to the Depression*. Cambridge, MA: Schenkman.

Lubove, Roy (1965). *The Professional Altruist: The Emergence of Social Work as a Career 1880–1930*. Cambridge, MA: Harvard University Press.

Lurie, Harry L. (1927). Specialized approaches to family case work. *Family, 8*, 202–205.

Lurie, Harry L. (1928a). Economic stabilization of the family: The standard of living. *Proceedings of the National Conference of Social Work, 55th Annual Session*. Chicago: University of Chicago Press.

Lurie, Harry L. (1928b). The case worker's aim in treating family discord. *Social Forces, 6*, 580–582.

Lurie, Harry L. (1931a). Discussion of Mr. Lee's paper. *Bulletin of the Welfare Council of New York City, 6*.

Lurie, Harry L. (1931b). The drift to public relief. *Proceedings of the National Conference Of Social Work, 58th Annual Session* (pp. 211–222). Chicago: University of Chicago Press.

Lurie, Harry L. (1931c). The place of federal aid in unemployment relief. *Social Service Review, 5*, 523–538.

Lurie, Harry L. (1931d). The Social Worker during the period of economic readjustment. Lecture notes, March 25. Lurie Papers, Box 2, Folder 14, University of Minnesota, National Social Welfare Archives Center.

Lurie, Harry L. (1931e). Review of *A Changing Psychology in Social Case Work*, by Virginia Robinson. *Social Service Review, 5*, 488.

Lurie, Harry L. (1932). Spreading relief thin. *Social Service Review, 6*, 223–234.

Lurie, Harry L. (1933a). A Program of National Assistance. Typewritten paper for a speech, December 9. Lurie Papers, Box 2, Folder 26, University of Minnesota, National Social Welfare Archives Center.

Lurie, Harry L. (1933b). Case work in changing order. *Survey, 69*, 61–64.

Lurie, Harry L. (1933c). Discussion of Helen Hall's paper on "Current American Methods of Handling Unemployed in the Light of Present Mental Hygiene Knowledge", typewritten, December 28., Lurie Papers, Box 1, Folder 10, University of Minnesota, National Social Welfare Archives Center.

Lurie, Harry L. (1933d). Letter to Harry L. Hopkins, November 17. Lurie Papers, Box 3, Folder 43, University of Minnesota, National Social Welfare Archives Center.

Lurie, Harry L. (1933e). Untitled paper dealing with unemployment, social work and the Depression, December 20. Lurie papers, Box 1, Folder 10, University of Minnesota, National Social Welfare Archives Center.

Lurie, Harry L. (1934). Letter from Lurie to Henry G. Leach, April 18,. (pp. 1–2).

Lurie Papers, Box 1, Folder 12, University of Minnesota, National Social Welfare Archives Center.

Lurie, Harry L. (1935a). Jane Addams. *Social Work Today, 2,* 17–18.

Lurie, Harry L. (1935b). The Social Worker and Reconstruction, Lecture notes, December 13. Lecture note card 1, Lurie Papers, Box 2, Folder 14, University of Minnesota, National Social Welfare Archives Center.

Lurie, Harry L. (1935c). The Dilemma of the Case Worker. *Social Work Today, 3,* 13–15.

Lurie, Harry L. (1938). Philosophy and Practice in Social Case Work, Typewritten, March 9. Lurie Papers, Box 4, Folder 72, University of Minnesota, National Social Welfare Archives Center.

Lurie, Harry L. (1946). The Next Twenty-Five Years, paper presented on October 28 to the St. Louis Chapter of the American Association of Social Workers. Lurie Papers, Box 3, Folder 29, University of Minnesota, National Social Welfare Archives Center.

Lurie, Harry L. (1949). Thought Control in Social Work and Related Fields, lecture notes for speech delivered April 7 at a Forum on Thought Control in Social Services, sponsored by SSEU. Lurie Papers, Box 3, Folder 29, University of Minnesota, National Social Welfare Archives Center.

Lurie, Harry L. (1960). The development of social welfare programs in the United States. *Social Work Yearbook* (14th ed.). New York: NASW.

Lurie, Harry L. (1961). *A Heritage Affirmed: The Jewish Federation Movement in America.* Philadelphia: Jewish Publication Society of America.

"Public Aid Asked in Welfare Work" (1932). *New York Times,* November 17, Lurie Papers, Box 2, Folder 26, University of Minnesota, National Social Welfare Archives Center.

Reynolds, Bertha Capen (1963). *An Uncharted Journey: Fifty Years of Growth in Social Work.* New York: Citadel.

Robinson, Virginia (1931). Letter to Lurie, November 12. Lurie Papers, Box 2, Folder 26, University of Minnesota, National Social Welfare Archive Center.

Schriver, Joe M. (1987a). Harry Lurie's assessment and prescription: An early view of social workers' roles and responsibilities regarding political action. *Journal of Sociology and Social Welfare, 14*(2), 11–127.

Schriver, Joe M. (1987b). Harry Lurie's critique: Person and environment in early casework practice. *Social Service Review, 61*(3), 514–532.

Smith, Dorothy W. (1937). Letter to Lurie, May 19. Lurie Papers, Box 3, Folder 52, University of Minnesota, National Social Welfare Archive Center.

Subcommittee on Future Coordination of Federal Dependency Relief Program (1934). Minutes of the meeting of the Subcommittee on Future Coordination of Federal Dependency Relief Program, Harry Lurie, Chair, January 17, p. 1. Lurie Papers, Box 1, Folder 3, University of Minnesota, National Social Welfare Archives Center.

"Transcript of the Luncheon Meeting" (1933). *Conference on National Economic Objectives for Social Work,* Harry Lurie, Chair, April 22. Lurie Papers, Box 1, Folder 7, University of Minnesota, National Social Welfare Archive Center.

Trattner, Walter I. (1974). *From Poor Law to Welfare State: A History of Social Welfare in America.* New York: Free Press.

9

Ideological Nostalgia, Intellectual Narcosis

DAVID STOESZ

For much of the past century, social work's orientation to social policy has been on the wrong side of history, in pursuit of a socialist welfare state. Toward the end of the Progressive era, American social workers struggled to respond to the dislocations of the Great Depression. Seduced by the romantic appeal of a European-style welfare state, social work rejected any accommodation to capitalism, opting instead for a democratic-socialist version of social policy that has pervaded social work's vision of social policy ever since. Using the social insurances established in the 1935 Social Security Act as exemplars, the American welfare state would inevitably, if gradually, introduce a corrective measure of socialism to the nation's political economy. Thus, with the welfare state as its icon, social work succumbed to ideological nostalgia, adopting a Marxist, historical determinism that preordained the inevitability of federal hegemony in social policy.

During the subsequent decades, American social work promoted state welfarism, insisting that universal entitlements were an unconditional right of citizenship, at the same time disparaging means-tested, public assistance programs. Voluntary sector initiatives were considered artifacts of an earlier era of social evolution; market strategies were antithetical to advancing the public welfare. So presumed, welfare state determinism became soporific, muffling the development of theory and research into social policy and programs. The result was intellectual narcosis; social work ceased generating substantive theory and conducting relevant research. As long as the American welfare state expanded, such navel-gazing on the part of social work was affordable. By the 1970s, however, a conservative assault on the welfare state was abetted by loss of public confidence in public welfare programs. Unwilling to entertain rival explanations to social welfare, social work stuck smugly to its welfare state

paradigm. Assuming the inevitable evolution of a complete array of entitlements, social work neglected to assess the experience of clients, the out-
comes of social programs, and public perception of the welfare state
project. By the mid-1990s, social work was utterly defenseless when conservatives began disassembling the welfare state.

A reconsideration of welfare capitalism is necessary if social work is to
attain relevancy in social policy. Three themes can reorient social work in
a neoprogressive era: accelerate the upward mobility of the poor, allow
consumers a choice of service provider, and deconstruct the welfare
bureaucracy. By advancing these themes, social work could be instrumental in the emergence of a postconservative policy environment.

IDEOLOGICAL NOSTALGIA

Social work's misdirection in social policy can be traced to the Progressive era. A particularly turbulent period, the Progressive era featured the
predations of industrial capitalism compounded by a massive influx of
immigrants who populated America's burgeoning cities. Progressives,
mostly well-educated, middle-income Protestants, focused their efforts on
regulating the excesses of industry, cleaning up municipal corruption, and
socializing immigrants to ideals of American citizenship. The precursors
of contemporary social work helped establish Charity Organization Societies, Settlements, and Children's Aid Societies as private ventures to further the Progressive movement. In so doing, early social activists used the
resources of philanthropically inclined capitalists to care for those who
were not "economically active and productive" (Katz, 1986, p. 13).

The Progressive legacy in social welfare would have been confined to
the voluntary sector's attempt to ameliorate urbanization and industrialization and a smattering of state welfare programs had it not been for the
economic collapse of 1929. Up to that point two models contended for the
allegiance of Progressive activists: welfare capitalism and welfare statism,
both of which are clearly evident in American social welfare today. Welfare
capitalism has its origins in the health, welfare, and retirement benefits
that industry included in wages for workers (Gilbert, 1983). Such benefits
were promoted heavily by American capitalists in order to attract more
capable employees. Speaking before the American Chamber of Commerce
in 1918, for example, John D. Rockefeller claimed that the benefits of welfare capitalism were so extensive as to reflect "the modern viewpoint" that
industry is "a form of social service" (Karger & Stoesz, 1997, p. 179). Welfare statism, on the other hand, drew its reference from the European
"social democratic model," which viewed the national government as the

source of essential protections against social and economic insecurity (Skocpol, 1992, pp. 26–30). According to welfare statism, the national government was a necessary corrective for the caprices of capitalism, the excesses of which at best generated chronic maldistribution of resources and at worst precipitated recessions.

Social work eventually adopted the welfare statist interpretation of social policy, in the process rejecting welfare capitalism and often vilifying the business sector. This is evident in Marti Bombyk's (1995) portrait of "progressive social work," a radical orientation to social welfare. Derived from a Marxist interpretation of political economy, progressive social work targets "capitalist economies that . . . enable concentrated wealth to accumulate into the hands of a small, elite group while most people receive far less" (p. 1933).

In response to the inability of government to counter the destabilizing tendencies of capitalism, progressive social workers align themselves with a labor movement "committed to advancing a socialist economic program that would replace the debilitated capitalist economy" (Bombyk, 1995, p. 1937). Presuming that welfare programs are deployed to placate the poor, progressive social workers not only criticize public assistance programs, but seek "social alternatives that prevent or mitigate poverty" and other problems (p. 1940). While Bombyk's characterization of progressive social work may be somewhat to the left of that eventually adopted by the profession, social work's profound skepticism—if not paranoia—toward capitalism was subsumed to enthusiasm about the much- celebrated federal welfare apparatus of welfare state ideology.

In its flirtation with left-wing ideology, social work has developed a curious antipathy toward capitalism. This is paradoxical in at least two respects. Foremost, the American liberalism to which most social workers would subscribe has always assumed the existence of a market economy and justified governmental intrusion only to advance the public interest. Moreover, private practice in social work relies on the market to provide service. Social workers in private practice may be petit capitalists, but they are no less capitalistic.

Regardless, social work students were taught that capitalism was contrary to social welfare because it skewed the distribution of resources, services, and opportunities resulting in poverty that was exacerbated by a host of corollary "-isms": racism, sexism, ageism. While this may have been true, it was also true that capitalism generated wealth, innovation, and spontaneity. Most social workers, to be certain, do not drive the government-issue automobile, live in a public housing project, obtain food from the public food warehouse, or seek entertainment by going out to see the government propaganda flick. Such alternatives have been tried by this and other national governments, and they have always been found wanting. Given the choice, the public (including social workers) opt to receive goods and services through the market.

Professional antipathy toward markets may be diminishing, however. As government reduces appropriations for discretionary programs, social workers are resorting to philanthropy for funding. Increasingly, foundations established by wealthy and altruistic individuals and corporations are an important resource for nonprofit organizations (Karger & Stoesz, 1997). Furthermore, innovations in service delivery often originate in the corporate sector and are transmitted by gurus such as Tom Peters, W. Edwards Deming, and Peter Drucker. Critics of the corporate sector might be asked to present comparable luminaries from the public sector, but the list would be short and dim. Arguably the most significant management book of the 1990s, a tome by David Osborne and Ted Gaebler, (1992) has a telling subtitle: *Reinventing Government: How the Entrepreneurial Spirit Is Transforming the Public Sector.*

The most significant implication of social work's ambivalence toward capitalism, however, is its failure to exploit the opportunities of the rapidly expanding health and human service corporations. As the human service sector of postindustrial society unfolds, what had once been public utilities during the industrial era are being converted into social markets. Firms now control substantial portions of markets in hospital management, HMOs, home health care, child day care, even corrections. Ever leery about doing much of anything with panache, social work has sat on the sidelines as corporate executives gobble up the new, expanding social markets. An increasing number of social workers are finding jobs in such firms and generally find the employment desirable; yet it is the rare social worker, indeed, who has the vision and gumption to set up a human service corporation.

Even social workers committed to (neo-)Marxism are being confronted with the following paradox. As of 1999, the Treasury Department is required to convert all federal payments from checks to electronic transfers. At current appropriation levels, federal welfare and Social Security benefits total about $500 billion. As of this writing almost one-fourth of that amount has been converted from checks to electronic transfer, meaning that beneficiaries have designated the financial institution to which their benefits are to be transmitted. Meanwhile states are converting to Electronic Benefit Transfer (EBT) for cash assistance and food stamps in order to save costs and reduce theft. In the absence of community-based financial institutions, virtually all of these deposits are going to commercial banks, which are profiting nicely from government EBT contracts. For example, each month state and federal governments deposit $29.7 million with First Security Bank in Utah to provide cash assistance and food stamps to poor families in New Mexico. On an annual basis that comes to more than one-quarter billion dollars in welfare benefits, and New Mexico is a relatively poor state. It requires little imagination to see how enterprising social workers could exploit provisions of the Community Development Banking and Financial Institutions Act of 1994 in order to create community development banks that could bid on EBT contracts, in the process securing millions of dollars for community development purposes. But that is unlikely so long as social work perceives capitalism as inconsistent with social welfare. That's not to say the EBT industry won't evolve, however. It will, and the profits of managing benefits for the poor will be diverted to financial managers and wealthy bankers. Given this opportunity, it's perverse to be Marxist!

Such contradictions notwithstanding, the welfare state has served as an icon for social work, an expectation that the national government would assure essential goods and services to the population as a right of citizenship. For most progressives, essential goods and services included employment, housing, health care, income, and the personal social services. According to the scenario, social progress was predestined: social policy would be the instrument for crafting a just society and progressive taxes would pay for it. Given the presumed inevitability of the formula, all American social workers had to do was beat the ideological drum; the welfare state was, after all, the final incarnation of industrial society. In a classic text, *Industrial Society and Social Welfare,* Harold Wilensky and Charles Lebeaux (1965) argued as much, writing that "under continuing industrialization all institutions will be oriented toward and evaluated in terms of social welfare aims. The 'welfare state' will become the 'welfare society,' and both will be more reality than epithet" (p. 127). American social workers who remained skeptical were directed to the English social philosopher Richard Titmuss, who suggested that the welfare state was boundless and would eventually become global, resulting in a "welfare world" (Titmuss, 1968, p. 127). In locating the American welfare state in the international context, James Midgley (1997) noted that "most scholars believe that the modern welfare state represents the culmination of an inevitable and desirable process of social evolution" (p. 441). Even in democratic-capitalist America, a "liberal welfare consensus as it became known dominated American life for many years" (p. 444).

In retrospect, such romanticism is a little naive. Yet, despite serious inconsistencies, it continued to guide social work in matters of social policy for decades. In its welfare state utopianism, social work erred in not recognizing that American social programs were located in a capitalist economy. Social Security, for example, mimicked private retirement funds already established by American business. In 1965, Medicare and Medicaid were structured to reimburse private providers for health care for the aged and poor (Karger & Stoesz, 1997). Later, when disenchantment grew with government provision of goods, such as employment (through the Concentrated Employment and Training Act) and housing (in the form of public housing projects constructed by the Department of Housing and Urban Development), federal initiatives were cashiered in favor of private sector alternatives. Despite such contradictions, social workers remained confident that the federal government would be the source of universal entitlements for the basic needs of Americans. For liberal social workers, the welfare state was not simply an exemplar, it had become an icon.

While the profession paid homage to the federal welfare state, many social workers voted with their feet, abandoning its programmatic manifestation, the public bureaucracy, for private practice. As Harry Specht and Mark Courtney (1994) observed, "In increasing numbers, social workers are flocking to psychotherapeutic pastures, hanging out their shingles to advertise themselves as psychotherapists just as quickly as licensing laws will permit" (p. 8). This was, of course, apostasy for welfare statists, who roundly condemned clinicians who became private practitioners. Instead of correctly placing this in the tradition of welfare capitalism, adherents of the welfare state brooked no quarter to those colleagues who retreated to the comfort, affluence, and facility of private clinical practice. Condemnation aside, clinicians departed the public sector in large numbers. Between 1988 and 1991, the number of NASW members who worked in private for-profit organizations increased from 19.8 to 23.8 percent, while those working in the public sector declined by a comparable percentage (Karger & Stoesz, 1997, p. 212).

Thus, ideological nostalgia for the European welfare state confounded American social work. While social work's policy gurus praised the virtues of public service for the welfare state, graduate students were running pell mell to the private sector. Instead of perceiving consumers as citizens, clinicians saw them as victims to be dealt with clinically, diagnosed as dysfunctional and treated with various medically related procedures (Best, 1997). Clinicians became skillful at exploiting the medical dysfunctions of its clients, in the process elevating its professional status and therapists' income. Regrettably, avarice frequently compromised professional ethics. Stuart Kirk and Herb Kutchins (1988) reported that "deliberate misdiagnosis" was a prevalent practice by social workers in private practice, and that 72 percent of social work respondents of their survey "were aware of cases where more serious diagnoses are used to qualify for reimbursement" (p. 235). Such opportunism was affordable so long as social work's clients were ignorant of unethical practices. Given the more substantive problem that clinical social work practice was effective at all, such ethical lapses were incidental, mere distractions in the course of going about one's professional business (Epstein, 1997). It was only a matter of time until insurance companies introduced corporate accountability to the scam through managed care, which called a halt to such nonsense. While social workers in private practice have whined about the intrusiveness of managed care on their professional prerogatives, they would be held in higher regard had they taken the high road and cleaned up their act first.

As a result of defection from the welfare state, social work eventually lost control of the welfare bureaucracy. Since passage of the Social Security Act, social work had been in charge of "the means of administration" for a range of income and social services (Gerth & Mills, 1974). During the next half-century, the federal and state departments of welfare were largely managed by social workers who exercised considerable influence, if not outright control, over public welfare. However, the work was not particularly engaging and eventually getting graduate-prepared social workers to work in public welfare was to become a chronic problem for public welfare administrators. This would prove fatal to social work's historic role as a leader in social policy. While the New Deal featured a pantheon of social workers (Frances Perkins, Harry Hopkins, the Abbott sisters, Julia Lathrop), the Great Society saw the numbers dwindle to a handful (Wilbur Cohen and Whitney Young, Jr.). By the Reagan era, there were no social workers of national repute to advance its policy agenda.

Without effective leadership, social work adopted a largely defensive posture vis-à-vis social policy. In some cases, the profession collaborated with other liberal groups to shoot down changes that were deemed harmful to the poor, such as Nixon's Family Assistance Plan, the last effort to establish a negative income tax in the United States. In other cases, social work negotiated dubious agreements that would later expose many of its traditional clients to abuse and neglect, as in the capping of appropriations for the Title XX Social Services program, while agreeing with the separation of services, which removed social workers from direct involvement with the welfare cash grant. In conjunction with passage of the Child Abuse Prevention and Treatment Act of 1974, this policy concession created the conditions for the scandals in child protection that would erupt nationwide within twenty years (Costin, Karger, & Stoesz, 1996). Regarding these policy decisions, it could be argued that social work actually worsened the circumstances of the welfare poor and vulnerable children subsequent to the War on Poverty.

THE CONSERVATIVE ASSAULT

Self-righteously confident in the welfare state icon, social workers remained oblivious of the conservative assault that was being planned on social welfare programs. While social work basked in Panglossian com-

placency, conservatives were busy cobbling together an intellectual infra-
structure that would not only challenge political liberalism but also shake
the foundations of its programmatic manifestation, the American welfare
state. The American Enterprise Institute recruited sociologist Peter Berger
and theologian Richard Neuhaus and commissioned them to write *To
Empower People: The Role of Mediating Structures in Public Policy* (Berger &
Neuhaus, 1977), a less than subtle critique of the welfare state. A Heritage
Foundation vice-president penned *Back to Basics* (Pines, 1982), a diatribe
against social programs and a paean to the family and private sector
approaches to social problems. The Manhattan Institute recruited Charles
Murray and paid him to write *Losing Ground* (1984), a shallow, but none-
theless effective critique of federal welfare policy. Lawrence Mead (1986)
contributed *Beyond Entitlement* to the conservative cause, and notes that
one of the reasons that liberal social programs were such ripe targets for
conservative sniping was that liberals had failed to do any new research
on poverty.

By the late 1980s, conservatives controlled the social policy debate.
Closeted safely in a fuzzy, reassuring philosophical cocoon, social work
was clueless about how this had come to happen. In fact, conservative cho-
reography of the media was so masterful that a nonacademic hack from
the Heritage Foundation, Robert Rector, was commonly featured in major
print and electronic media stories on welfare issues. By contrast, social
work was lost in the woods, shouting to gain the ear of reporters. At a
meeting on welfare reform urgently called by the National Association of
Social Workers in the mid-1990s, few social work scholars and staff could
recognize Rector's name, even though he had been featured on the front
page of that morning's edition of the *Washington Post* in a feature story on
welfare reform (author's observation).

Around the ideological corner, insurgents were planning an internal
coup for the Democratic party. Chastened by presidential election losses of
Walter Mondale and Michael Dukakis, neoliberal insurgents maneuvered
the party away from the political left toward the center. Instrumental in
this was Al From, a veteran Democrat who became the director of the
Democratic Leadership Council (DLC), which later spun off a think tank,
the Progressive Policy Institute, to generate neoliberal ideas for Democratic candidates. Elected officials who led the DLC included the governor of
Arkansas, Bill Clinton, and a senator from Tennessee, Al Gore. Once Clinton and Gore had triumphed in the Democratic primary, From crowed that
the DLC had taken the Democratic party away from the poor, minorities,
women, and gays (briefing, DLC headquarters attended by the author).
Having secured the presidency, Clinton's antiliberal instincts began to sur-
face, particularly after the health reform debacle (Stoesz, 1996). Sheepishly,
social work was reluctant to criticize the Clinton administration; after two

Republican presidents, the Arkansas Democrat had to be an improvement. While social work clung to Clinton during his reelection campaign, few human service professionals seemed to recognize that voting Democratic was not for a second term for Clinton but actually a fifth term of the Reagan presidency.

By the late 1990s, social program debris attributable to attacks on the welfare state could not be dismissed. In 1989 Catastrophic Health Insurance was repealed by Congress, the first retraction of a social insurance program in the history of the American welfare state. During the first Clinton term, the Health Security Act failed despite its having been drafted as probusiness legislation; a more liberal California initiative crafted along the Canadian single-payer model also lost by a substantial margin. Then, on August 22, 1996, President Clinton signed the Personal Responsibility and Work Opportunity Reconciliation Act (PRWORA), capping expenditures for poor families, devolving welfare to the states, introducing a five-year lifetime limit on public assistance, and denying welfare to legal immigrants. While social worker professional organizations voiced their objections to "welfare reform," NASW later expressed relief that child welfare had not been similarly block-granted and devolved to the states, even though the PRWORA cut in the Title XX program exceeded any additional allocations for child welfare. Having been excused from the table, social work was reduced to exclaiming over those crumbs that remained after the gluttons had departed.

INTELLECTUAL NARCOSIS

Deluded into thinking that the welfare state had an ineluctable appeal that would portend its elaboration to Northern European proportions, social workers failed to generate theory and research about social policy and programs. Initially, the profession justified its failure to engage in original thought citing eclecticism. Given the emphasis of clinical practice, social work resorted to schemes developed by psychiatry and psychology, the *Diagnostic and Statistical Manual* eventually becoming the coda for clinical social workers. In matters relating to poverty, social work conceded the field of quantitative analysis to social scientists, primarily economists. That serious thought had anything to do with the social work project seemed irrelevant so long as social welfare expanded and the profession could lift ideas from other disciplines. For much of the twentieth century, this proved the case. Even when radical academics, such as Jeffrey Galper and Richard Cloward, or activists, such as Saul Alinsky, uncovered the charade, these proved nuisances that passed with time. Nonplused and inert, social work consolidated its institutional credentials; the National

Association of Social Worker's "edifice complex" surfaced with its construction of a new building in the nation's capital, the Council on Social Work Education moved into a toney address not far away in suburban Virginia.

Rather than take its intellectual work seriously, social work defined itself as a derivative activity dependent on other disciplines for knowledge. This was convenient in that it avoided "thinking theory" and "doing research," activities that had become somewhat rigorous as the academic and applied disciplines evolved. And it avoided the internecine squabbles that surfaced in disciplines in which competing schools of thought and procedure developed. Always disconcerted by dissension, social work found solace in ambiguous notions, such as "person-in-environment," sought refuge in inferior methods, such as "single-subject design," and waxed solipsistic about the "strengths perspective"—formulations that would be considered primitive, if not laughable, by other disciplines. (Would you consent to an operation by a surgeon whose identification was the "health perspective"?)

Later, social work defended its inferior thinking on the basis that its reality was not amenable to conventional methods of investigation. This is simply untenable. When social work does seek an intellectual justification for its activities, it is quick to resort to the theory and research of other disciplines. Furthermore, other professions, such as public health and criminology, contend with social realities as sticky as social work's and they still generate substantive theory and conduct state-of-the-art research. Yet social work has gone its own way and with predictable consequences: its research is so inadequate that in 1988 the director of the National Institute of Mental Health was provoked to goad social work to come up to speed with other human service disciplines in generating knowledge (Austin, 1992, pp. 311–322). Compared to the substantial research literature that has been generated by the teaching and nursing professions, occupational groups that also trace their origins to the Progressive era, that social work should require such prodding is nothing less than humiliating.

Public welfare and child welfare provide specific, if excruciating, examples of the profession's failure in research. Even though social work has been involved in public welfare since its inception, its research efforts began to lag after the New Deal. Content to rely on the sporadic data generated by state and federal bureaucracies, the profession neglected to develop an independent research capacity.[1] Subsequently, social work unwittingly fell in line with the welfare status quo, and it was probably just a matter of time until the profession diverged from the social reality of recipients (whose experience no one had bothered to sample), the public (who had increasing misgivings about welfare), even welfare caseworkers (who were abandoning the bureaucracy).

Perhaps social work's greatest fault has been its maintenance of the public welfare bureaucracy. During the past two decades, the nation has seen a variety of innovations in what had once been public utilities. In health care, HMOs have redirected resources away from curative and rehabilitative medicine, toward prevention. In education, magnet schools, charter schools, and vouchers have been introduced to make education more responsive to poor families. But none of this has happened in public welfare. Contrary to the experimentation that defines contemporary organizations from the public and private sector, the welfare department endures, the last vestige of state socialism in America.

That the welfare bureaucracy has detrimental features is not particularly newsworthy. Almost *two decades* ago, sociologist Michael Lipsky (1984) coined the term "bureaucratic disentitlement" to describe the tendency of welfare workers to deny benefits to citizens eligible for assistance. The culture of the welfare department meant that "workers on the front lines of the welfare state find themselves in a corrupted world of service. [They] find that the best way to keep demand within manageable proportions is to deliver a consistently inaccessible or inferior product" (Lipsky, 1984, p. xiii). A revolution may have occurred in organization theory since Lipsky's observations, but none of it trickled down to the local welfare department. In 1993, a journalist sketched this portrait of a Los Angeles welfare office:

> Welfare offices are so understaffed, the workers so burnt out, that some help applicants cheat just to fill unofficial quotas, avoid confrontation, get them out of their hair. It is a system so flawed that the greedy, the lazy, rip and run with ease. The attitude of both sides of the reinforced windows that separate staff from applicants is: Us against Them. The system becomes so cynical that the desperate—the great majority of applicants, by most estimates—are left under a pall of suspicion, clawing even harder to get the help to which they're entitled. (Goodman, 1993, p. 30)

Of course, such conditions are likely to worsen as a result of capping welfare and devolving it to the states, a replication of the disaster that has befallen child welfare. Public welfare, any graduate social work student could tell you, is at the bottom of the prospective employment list of most freshly minted MSWs. To entice new graduate social workers to the public sector, training grants are available through Title VI-E of the Social Security Act, yet this strategy is largely self-defeating. In the absence of major structural reform of the welfare bureaucracy, the IV-E trainees are being recruited to an organizational purgatory that no capable professional could endure for long. Few do. Most trainees view the grant as a temporary assignment: a convenient way to secure the two years of MSW supervision required for full-status licensure, then it's *adios* to the welfare bureaucracy.

In some respects, public welfare administrators cannot be held responsible for the oppressive bureaucracies that impede the delivery of professional quality human services; the responsibility resides with the schools of social work and the accrediting authority that oversees their curricula, the Council on Social Work Education. Even graduate programs in social administration fail to require even elementary courses in accounting; more sophisticated information systems are beyond the comprehension of most faculty. By comparison, such courses are common in graduate programs in education and health administration. Is it any wonder then, when confronted by an elected official who demands innovations that might make the local welfare department more effective, the department director retreats to old shibboleths about high caseloads, poorly educated/trained staff, and inadequate benefits? Such excuses may do in a pinch, but they founder when managers from other disciplines examine public welfare; where social work administrators see intransigence, contemporary human service managers see opportunity. To date, two states—Texas and New Jersey—are planning to privatize entire chunks of the welfare bureaucracy. Given the apparent intractability of the welfare bureaucracy, elected officials will continue to insist that administrators conceive of innovations. If they are unable to produce strategies that are comparable to those of managers in other industrial sectors, the result is likely to be wholesale privatization. Once that occurs, there is no guarantee that social work will have an even remote influence in public welfare.

A convenient illustration of the absurdities with which social work became associated was the welfare error-rate, the percentage of incorrect payments that can result in federal penalties to state welfare agencies. Public welfare administrators claimed that error-rates were below 5 percent in order to avoid federal penalties, and social work texts used this figure to refute one of the "myths" of welfare: that most recipients cheat. Social work continued this delusion until Kathryn Edin and Christopher Jencks produced research showing that more than 95 percent of payments were incorrect because recipients had significant unreported income (as a result of trying to compensate for deteriorating benefits) that was not reported to welfare officials (Edin & Jencks, 1992). Social work, in other words, was defending a position that was not simply wrong, it was diametrically opposed to reality—a reality that the profession might have understood more adequately, given its five-decade proximity to welfare and poverty, had it taken the trouble to conduct independent research on poor families.

Since the Family Support Act of 1988, research on welfare reform has focused on the employment prospects of poor mothers. As a result of federal waivers granted to the states and considerable interest by the philanthropic community, many studies have been undertaken on problems low- income mothers experience when they are forced into the labor market (Stoesz, 1997). Most of this research has been conducted by private organizations, such as the Manpower Demonstration Research Corporation, Abt Associates, and Mathematica, using government data and much of it is deficient (Epstein, 1997). Given its historical concern for the poor and its contemporary interest in the feminization of poverty, social work would have been well-suited to counter the official celebrations of progress in welfare reform with perspectives of poor mothers, including their perceptions as well as experiences with public assistance and work. Yet such research appears only episodically, certainly not as a consistent demonstration of the profession's concern for poor mothers and their children.

Child welfare provides another, more tragic illustration. Social work has had primary responsibility for child welfare for more than a century, pioneering a number of innovations that were considered at the time as alternatives to harmful families and malevolent institutions. As was the case in public welfare, however, child welfare professionals failed to undertake serious research on the welfare of children and the context of child welfare. As a result, child welfare policy of the past two decades has lurched from bad to worse, resulting in social workers rationing care for maltreated children while protecting a disintegrating child welfare "system." Much of the current travails in child welfare can be dated from 1974, when the Child Abuse and Treatment Act mandated reporting of child abuse and neglect, and the Title XX Social Services program was capped at $2.5 billion. Subsequently, reports of maltreatment skyrocketed, but states failed to compensate for the federal failure to increase appropriations. Soon, children were being shuffled into foster care and experiencing multiple placements, but child welfare professionals were losing their grasp on what continued to be referred to euphemistically as the "child welfare system." In order to stabilize children, the 1980 Adoption Assistance and Child Welfare Act mandated "permanency planning." Without adequate funding, however, this became illusory, as Theodore Stein was to observe several years later: "Many states did not know how many children they had in care nor where the children were placed. Regularly scheduled case review was the exception, and when it did occur, it often consisted of little more than a rubber-stamping procedure" (Stein, 1987, p. 643). Such administrative ineptitude would eventually result in child welfare agencies in twenty-one states and the District of Columbia being placed under court administration.

Confronted with increased demand and static resources, child welfare workers settled on "family preservation" as an alternative to out-of-home placement. Early enthusiasm for family preservation might have dimmed when the few experimental studies conducted to examine the innovation suggested that children receiving family preservation interventions fared no better than those receiving traditional protective services, but child welfare professionals disregarded the research. Desperate for an alternative method to out-of-home placement that would conserve dwindling resources, child welfare professionals embraced family preservation even when anecdotal evidence suggested that abused children were further endangered and died after they were returned to unsafe parents (Costin, Karger, & Stoesz, 1996). Despite enthusiasm for family preservation, by the early 1990s the situation had worsened. Edith Fein and Anthony Maluccio (1992) noted, "The children's agencies in each state are overwhelmed by the number of cases, caseworkers are inadequately trained and responsible for too many children, and the resources for assisting families (such as public housing, prenatal care, and drug- treatment programs) are insufficient for the demand" (p. 337). Of the future of child welfare, Fein and Maluccio projected "overwhelming crisis" (ibid.).

When the murders of children such as Lisa Steinberg and Elisa Izquierdo in New York City became front-page news, child welfare professional retreated behind confidentiality to protect a child welfare nonsystem that had all but ceased functioning. In the course of researching a story on child homicide, journalists Rochelle Sharpe and Marjie Lundstrom contacted state child welfare administrators to determine child fatalities, but were told the data either were not available or were protected by confidentiality laws (the former a result of administrative incompetence, the latter a convenient misunderstanding of privacy protections). Not dissuaded, Sharpe and Lundstrom hired their own researcher, examined data tapes from the Centers for Disease Control, and wrote a story, "Getting Away with Murder," that won a Pulitzer Prize in 1990. In recalling the experience, Lundstrom concluded that child welfare administrators were more interested in protecting their bureaucratic fiefdoms than children who had died from neglect and abuse (Costin, Karger, & Stoesz, 1996).

A NEOPROGRESSIVE FUTURE

For social work to regain footing on such rapidly eroding terrain, the profession should reconsider its antipathy to markets, dust off welfare capitalism, and insert it as the profession's orientation to social policy. It goes without saying that social work must begin to generate its own theory and conduct its own research in social policy, including program outcome studies as well as modeling innovations in social policy. Accordingly, three themes should guide social work in future social policy:

(1) Accelerate the Upward Mobility of the Poor: Virtually all income and in-kind assistance for the poor and vulnerable is in the form of mini-

mal support, the notion being that people will eventually pull themselves out of poverty. While this has a virtuous ring for most conservatives, it is of marginal benefit to poor families given their circumstances. Most poor heads-of-household are either involved in the labor market or want to be, but the inadequacy of low-wage jobs condemns them to running in place ever more rapidly in the squirrel cage of marginal employment (Spalter-Roth, Burr, & Hartmann, 1995). The poor who do escape poverty do so by accruing assets. This is, of course, what Asian-Americans have been doing so successfully, replicating what Jews did generations before, making them among the most successful immigrant groups. Most professional social workers expect to do the same, so it is particularly disingenuous that they would fail to generate comparable opportunities for the families they serve.

Michael Sherraden (1991), one of the bright spots in American social work, has studied the welfare poor and conceived of Individual Development Accounts (IDAs) to accelerate their upward mobility. IDAs are tax-exempt accounts that can be used for finishing college or vocational school, buying a home, establishing a business, or supplementing a pension; the amount contributed is matched by a formula according to the income of the account-holder (Sherraden, 1991). Although the federal welfare reform legislation should be denounced on several counts, like most legislation it includes some laudable provisions, in this case IDAs. But the PRWORA-IDA provision, unlike child day care, includes no particular appropriation, so social workers who want to boost the welfare poor out of the underclass using an asset-based strategy must draw from existing revenues. Given the ubiquity of ideological nostalgia and its suspicion of anything that verges on capital accumulation and individual initiative, social workers may come to IDAs eventually, but if they do, the affinity will be glacial in its evolution, crystallizing sometime before the next ice age, perhaps.

Insofar as social work depends on income support and avoids capital accumulation as poverty reduction strategies, the profession condemns thousands of poor families to chronic poverty. After five decades of experience with poverty programs, it is shameful that the profession has failed to recognize this sooner, as embarrassing as it has been to have conservative ideologues blast social work for aggravating the dependence of the poor on poverty programs. Is it possible these are related—that social work's insistence on income support programs and its negation of asset accrual strategies of poverty alleviation do, in effect, consign the poor to dependence on welfare programs? Interestingly, the more successful development programs in the Third World, such as the Grameen Development Bank and Habitat for Humanity, eschew public charity, insisting that the poor contribute to their own well-being (Stoesz, Guzzetta, & Lusk,

1999). While social work persists in defending outmoded income support programs, the newest thinking in poverty remediation is around micro-credit, peer lending, sweat equity—all asset-based strategies.

(2) Allow Consumers the Choice of Service Provider: Nowhere is social work more duplicitous than what it expects of poor Americans. In search of goods and services, affluent citizens shop on the market; only the poor are shunted to public welfare departments. Ask a typical social worker if she would consult the income maintenance division of the local welfare department for help in financial planning or seek the aid of social services staff with a personal problem, and the response is laughter. It is indeed preposterous to expect the middle class to rely on the welfare bureaucracy, but that is what we require of the poor. This is stated eloquently by Theresa Funicello, a former public assistance recipient:

> When affluent people decide some service they want for themselves isn't up to snuff, they vote with their feet and their pocketbooks. In that sense, markets work quite well for anyone with the power to participate in them. As long as poor people are prohibited from having a choice—a say in deciding which services they need and which providers are most capable of satisfying them—the competitive element, if there is one, is entirely in the hands of Big Brother. Most of the people in every form of this business know this: there is no accountability in the social service field. None demanded, none supplied. (Funicello, 1993, p. 252)

The profession's rebuttal to such accusations has been an implicit assumption that the poor are incapable of selecting what they need from the market, and that public social welfare provides goods and services for which no markets exist. If this were true and if social welfare were accountable to the poor, social work would have at least sampled the perceptions of welfare recipients about the services they receive. That the profession has failed to develop any longitudinal research on recipients' experience with public welfare is one of its most blatant omissions, leaving the profession vulnerable to conservative accusations that the true purpose of public welfare is not to provide meaningful assistance to the poor, but to employ social workers.

The most direct way to introduce choice in social welfare would be to allow recipients to designate the financial institution to which they which they want their income benefits transmitted and to make social service vouchers available with which recipients can shop for services on the market. By allowing designation of cash benefits, recipients would be able to use the financial services of institutions that are used by the middle class, such as commercial banks and credit unions. By introducing vouchers, the poor could take advantage of private service providers, and vouchers would further expand that portion of the market that serves poor families.

Of course, social workers tend to blanch at such suggestions. The predictable response of ideological nostalgiacs is to chronicle the negative features of markets, as if these somehow justify the maintenance of the public welfare bureaucracy. To be sure, markets are not panaceas; but so long as they are preferred by the vast majority of Americans—certainly most social workers—they can respond to the choices of the poor as well.

(3) Deconstruct the Welfare Bureaucracy: Among the indicators of social work's divergence from mainstream America, none are quite as revealing as the tales of Kimi Gray and "Polly" Williams. Kimi Gray was a welfare mother living in a Washington, D.C., public housing project that had become infested with drug dealers. On her own, she organized her neighbors, ejected the drug peddlers, then suggested that her tenants' group purchase their housing units, the assumption being that owner-occupied housing was better maintained than traditional, rented public housing. This captured the attention of then-HUD Secretary Jack Kemp, who initiated a program that transferred the ownership of public housing units to renters. "Polly" Williams was a Milwaukee welfare mother who had impeccable liberal credentials, having led Jesse Jackson's presidential campaigns in the city. Disenchanted with the status quo, she sought and won a seat in the state legislature from which she launched a program to make public education more accountable to parents such as herself. Williams's voucher program for poor families, pioneered in Milwaukee, attracted the attention of then-secretary of education William Bennett, who promoted vouchers as a way to reform public education. Bennett and Kemp drew on these experiences to establish a new think tank, Empower America (Stoesz, 1996). Note that, in both instances, minority welfare mothers empowered themselves, came to the attention of movement conservatives, who then capitalized on the leadership of Gray and Williams to further the objectives of the political Right.

The courage and imagination of Gray and Williams could have been instrumental in reviving an ossifying liberalism, of course, and social workers might have been instrumental in that revitalization, but the profession was so wedded to the public welfare bureaucracies of the welfare state that it was unthinkable to "privatize" them. After all, if the bureaucracies of public housing and public education were deconstructed, would public welfare be far behind?

Precisely!

Having experimented with health care and education, a variety of methods are available to deconstruct the welfare bureaucracy. Obviously, allowing recipients choice in the provision of income and social service benefits would dismantle much of it. A particularly interesting variation would be to introduce reimbursement by capitation, an arrangement through which private service providers would be paid according to the number of poor families they serve. Lousy service would result in families departing inferior providers in search of better service; better providers would advertise for members and evolve plans that suit the particular needs of member families. Crummy providers would wither while more effective ones would thrive. A midway strategy would allow groups of professionals and consumers to charter their own human service agencies just as many states allow teachers and parents to charter schools. Unaccountably, virtually none of these options are given serious consideration within the public welfare literature.

*   *   *   *   *   *

The end of the century is a propitious time to reorient social work vis-à-vis social policy. E. J. Dionne, Jr., has proposed "neoprogressivism" as the tonic for a dyspeptic liberalism. According to Dionne, the "end of big government" reflects the irrelevance of welfare state liberalism in contemporary politics. Much as the old Progressive movement signaled the end of industrial-era, cowboy capitalism in America, neoprogressivism represents the replacement of an unrestrained federal government with accelerating upward mobility, maintaining economic expansion, and reducing social and economic inequality. In securing these objectives, however, neoprogressives eschew the mechanics of big government: "[A]ll neoprogressives are open to experimentation and to the reform and reconstruction of the public sector" (Dionne, 1996, p. 336). In addition to calling for a reevaluation of its alignment with the welfare state, neoprogressivism suggests a reassessment of the profession's historical understanding of progressivism.

Although social work has much ground to make up if it is to be taken seriously in the rapidly evolving human service sector of postindustrial America, what may be its final opportunity will become evident within the next decade. Corporate rationing of human services through managed care coupled with bureaucratic rationing of welfare benefits through welfare reform will generate severe dislocations—a "crisis" in social work parlance—and interest will build for alternative arrangements for helping the vulnerable poor. By now a fairly extensive list of options for revitalization has evolved, but this will be of little avail if social work continues its indulgence in ideological nostalgia. A social work that is incompetent in research, paranoid about capitalism, and protective of archaic welfare bureaucracies will not prosper. On the other hand, a neoprogressive effort to accelerate the upward mobility of the poor, allow them choice in service provision, while dismantling the welfare bureaucracy would have significant and multiple benefits. Poor consumers would know that their perceptions were being respected; the public would appreciate the profession's willingness to make taxpayers' resources more accountable;

and politicians would perceive social work and the programs it manages as being an integral component of community development. Having shed its allegiance to antiquated values, social work could be once again what it had been in the halcyon days of Jane Addams, Harry Hopkins, and Wilbur Cohen, a beacon for social justice in America.

NOTE

1. The University of Wisconsin Institute for Research on Poverty is an exception. It is unfair to expect one institution to compensate for the inadequacy of an entire profession.

REFERENCES

Austin, D. (1992). Findings of the NIMH task force on social work research. *Research on Social Work Practice, 2*(3), 311–322.

Berger, P. & Neuhaus, R. (1977). *To Empower People*. Washington: American Enterprise Institute.

Best, J. (1997). Victimization and the victim industry. *Society, 34*(4).

Bombyk, M. (1995). Progressive social work. *Encyclopedia of Social Work* (19th ed., pp. 1933–1942). Washington, DC: NASW Press.

Costin, L., Karger, H., & Stoesz, D. (1996). *The Politics of Child Abuse in America*. New York: Oxford University Press.

Dionne, E. (1996). *They Only Look Dead*. New York: Simon and Schuster.

Edin, K., & Jencks, C. (1992). Reforming welfare. In C. Jencks, *Rethinking Social Policy* (pp. 204–235). Cambridge, MA: Harvard University Press.

Epstein, W. (1997). *Welfare in America*. Madison: University of Wisconsin Press.

Fein, E., & Maluccio, A. (1992). Permanency planning: Another remedy in jeopardy. *Social Service Review, 66*(3), 335–348.

Funicello, T. (1993). *Tyranny of Kindness*. New York: Atlantic Monthly.

Gerth, H., & Mills, C. W. (1974). *Max Weber: Essays in Sociology*. New York: Oxford University Press.

Gilbert, N. (1983). *Capitalism and the Welfare State*. New Haven, CT: Yale University Press.

Goodman, M. (1993). Just another day in paradise. *Los Angeles Times Magazine*, December 19, p. 30.

Karger, H., & Stoesz, D. (Eds.) (1997). *American Social Welfare Policy* (3rd ed.). New York: Longman. Katz, M. (1986). *In the Shadow of the Poorhouse*. New York: Basic Books.

Kirk, S. , & Kutchins, H. (1988). Deliberate misdiagnosis in mental health practice. *Social Service Review, 62*, 225–237. Lipsley, M. (1984). Bureaucratic disentitlement in social welfare programs. *Social Service Review, 33*(4), 81–88.

Lusk, M., Guzzetta, C., & Stoesz, D. (1999). *International Development*. Boston: Allyn and Bacon.

Mead, Lawrence (1986). *Beyond Entitlement.* New York: Free Press.

Midgley, James (1997). The American welfare state in international perspective. In H. Karger and D. Stoesz (Eds.), *American Social Welfare Policy* (3rd ed., pp. 434–449). New York: Longman.

Murray, Charles (1984). *Losing Ground.* New York: Basic Books. Osborne, D., & Gaebler, T. (1992). *Reinventing Government.* Reading, MA: Addison-Wesley.

Pines, B. (1982). *Back to Basics.* New York: William Morrow.

Sherraden, Michael (1991). *Assets and the Poor.* Armonk: M. E. Sharpe.

Skocpol, T. (1992). *Protecting Soldiers and Mothers.* Cambridge, MA: Harvard University Press.

Spalter-Roth, R., Burr, B., & Hartmann, H. (1995). *Welfare That Works.* Washington, DC: Institute for Women's Policy Research.

Specht, Harry, & Courtney, Michael (1994). *Unfaithful Angels.* New York: Free Press.

Stein, T. (1987). Foster care for children. *Encyclopedia of Social Work* (18th ed., pp. 639–650). Washington: NASW Press.

Stoesz, David (1996). *Small Change: Domestic Policy under the Clinton Presidency.* White Plains: Longman.

Stoesz, David (1997). Welfare behaviorism. *Society, 34*(3), 68–77.

Stoesz, David, Guzzetta, C., & Lusk, M. (1999). *International Development.* Boston: Allyn & Bacon.

Titmuss, Richard (1968). *Commitment to Welfare.* New York: Pantheon.

Wilensky, H., & Lebeaux, C. (1965). *Industrial Society and Social Welfare.* New York: Free Press.

Afterword

CLARKE A. CHAMBERS

Over the years I have learned that there are no set models or formulas for the composition of an Afterword. Some seek to summarize major themes emerging from separate pieces in an anthology. Some veer off in new directions with but little reference to what has gone before. Some provide focused analysis of select sections that happen to be within the critic's realm of personal expertise. Some are largely complimentary; others are gratuitously argumentative.

In the meandering comments that follow, I intend to follow none of these styles exclusively and draw a bit from each. I do *not* propose to set down another monographic analysis. I propose, rather, to provide an eclectic, subjective running commentary on what I perceive to be the central issues addressed by others in this important volume—among them the shifting concern of professional social workers regarding poverty and the needs of the poor in the United States over the past century. If at times I seem to slip away from that focus, I can only plea for patience from the reader. I have purposefully set aside the scholarly apparatus of precise footnote citations—emeritus status should carry some privileges not generally permitted to active career academics. In short, I conceive of this Afterword as constituting an informal reflective essay.

In many ways, the contributors to this challenging volume express their dismay at the apparent failure of professional social work to remain true to its presumed originating mission to understand the root causes of social poverty, then to seek to alleviate and perhaps finally to eliminate the existence of poverty in a society dedicated to material progress; and in the meantime to provide appropriate services and assistance to those unhappy citizens who suffered the consequences of conditions not of their own making. The forces that led social workers to drift away from that initial cause are explored in these chapters: a growing, and increasingly narrow focus on creating "professional" career lines for human service workers; the intellectual seduction of psychology and varied schools of psychoanalysis that proved heady, rewarding, and finally distracting; a failure of professional leaders and associations, especially in the 1930s, to incorporate public welfare agents, most of them lacking certification, into established norms, institutions, and education, and thus to achieve control over the supply of social servants; the implicit racism of practicing social workers that kept agency programs separated from clienteles of color, and distanced therefore from those groups that suffered poverty disproportionately. In one degree and another these explanations have about them a plausible and even persuasive logic.

It may be, however, that the pioneer generation of social workers, ca. 1890–1920, were not as united in a crusade for progressive measures as heroic historical accounts of social work's foremothers and forefathers have made out. We are nostalgic for figures who manifested a devotion to social justice in that exciting era (exciting, that is, to scholars and practitioners of liberal, social democratic proclivities). Jane Addams, Florence Kelley, Paul Kellogg, the Abbott sisters, and their goodly company did indeed contribute to the construction of analyses that traced poverty to social conditions and economic structures rather than to moral and behavioral shortcomings of those who were poor. In those efforts they are allied with a number of reformers—economists Richard T. Ely and John R. Commons, social gospel theologians such as Walter Rauschenbusch and George Herron, progressive Catholic leaders, most notably Father John Ryan, proponent of a "living wage" standard for family income (later in life dubbed Monsignor New Deal), muckraking journalists and novelists, and ultimately a number of politicians at every level of government. Prominent social work leaders and educators, most effectively a cadre of settlement house head residents, constituted important elements in these reform coalitions. Associations dedicated to reform included many figures less notable than Jane Addams. The National Child Labor Committee, the National Consumers' League, the Association for Labor Legislation, the Urban League, and similar groups all constituted coalitions of dedicated citizens, among others ministers, journalists, academic scholars, lawyers, enlightened business leaders, educators and teachers . . . and persons identified with emerging careers in social service.

Later other groups and associations would gain prominence in such social movements—organized labor, especially the CIO, became a powerful force in the elaboration of public policies related to issues broadly defined as centered on human welfare during the Roosevelt New Deal era and again during the Lyndon Johnson years. Social Security, minimum wage, progressive taxation, housing, public health, and the Civil Rights and Voting Rights Acts of the mid-1960s. Medicaid and Medicare all gained authority by the exertion of political clout by organized labor, allied with like-minded pressure groups and organized citizens, including spokespersons from professional social work, now junior partners where earlier they had enjoyed senior status.

It was also the case, however, that at the beginning of this century, a host of practitioners in agencies that in time would be identified as "social work" went about their daily tasks without engaging themselves actively in movements aimed at the elimination of conditions that reformers identified as root causes of social poverty. The settings in which they worked included associated charities, settlements and neighborhood centers, youth-serving agencies, schools, hospitals and clinics, travelers' aid, city missions, orphanages, old people's homes, disaster relief, and the courts— to name but a few places in which social services were practiced. Many of their clients were indeed poor—but services of alleviation understandingly and appropriately took precedence over engagement in crusades for social justices. I suspect that concentration on service has continued to be the case for persons engaged in all sorts of social service over the years and still at the cusp of the millennium. Just like other professionals—lawyers, doctors, dentists, engineers, architects, musicians, and folks who kick, hit, catch, and throw balls, whatever the occupation or career—social workers attended to daily responsibilities and tasks without major concern about larger social or cultural matters.

Surely it has also been true that in season and out, during times favorable to reform and times of stability or reaction, representatives of the professions have appeared before city councils, county boards of supervisors, and state legislative committees to bear witness to the concerns for the less fortunate who are among their clients. Ordinances and legislative acts are constantly under review; public officials recurrently propose extension of programs or their retraction. The tinkering never ceases. Giving testimony is often a tedious and thankless task, but social workers and associations have persisted in presenting evidence arising from their practice. The path of social policy has been more often incremental (or decremental) than marked by sudden lurches forward or backward. Such processes are not as dramatic as the enactment in 1935 of the Social Security Act, for example, and they have not, therefore, attracted the attention of historians. It is a story generally neglected by scholars. The records are difficult to locate and (let us be frank) they are tedious to study; but I suspect that what I have observed here in Minnesota over the past several decades is not peculiar to this progressive state alone. Practicing social workers of modest means and attainment continue to express in a variety of venues their determination to seek remedy for the plight of the disadvantaged, even though their energies are primarily consumed in practice. Rarely have such persons carried the visibility or clout of a Grace Abbott or a Mary Van

Kleeck or a Harry Lurie, but at a grass-roots (or asphalt pavement) level they have remained faithful in their way to those who carried the banner fifty or one hundred years ago. A saving remnant of human services practitioners never deserted the poor.

Returning briefly to the era historians have labeled as "Progressive," it may be salutary to note in passing, as several chapters here detail, that professional welfare leaders were sharply divided on the viability and value of mothers' assistance programs, enacted in nearly every state during the decade 1910–1920. Florence Kelley and her allies spoke most forcibly for legislation that would provide financial assistance to needy mothers without regard to criteria of "morals" or behavior; to her and to others the assistance should come as of right, as legal entitlement. Social workers out of Charity Organization Society movement held other views. They feared the inefficiency and lack of accountability inherent in public assistance as they knew it, and insisted on administrative rules that would honor criteria of "less eligibility" and "suitable home." Charity workers carried the day. Morals test were strictly applied, and benefits were always below a level of health and decency; only a small proportion of those statistically in need were ever enrolled: women of color were almost universally excluded from eligibility.

A related observation needs to be inserted. Taking the long view, America moved reluctantly, in jerks and starts, toward the elaboration of a partial welfare state, particularly when contrasted with states in Western Europe, but times for effective national action proved to be relatively brief. Progressive child labor legislation, at state and national levels, was struck down by the courts, and not constitutionally affirmed until the late 1930s. The goals of mothers' assistance were subverted by legislative rules and administrative implementation. After the enactment of emergency measures to soften the impact of hard times, the New Deal had but four years or so, 1935–1939, to enact Social Security, categorical aids, work relief, the right of labor to organize and bargain collectively through agents of its own choosing (over time an effective strategy to raise wages and improve conditions), fair labor standards, and minimum wage and maximum hour rules. LBJ's proclaimed "War on Poverty"—civil rights, voting rights, Medicare, Medicaid, "maximum feasible participation" of the poor in poverty programs—all came in two or three years, 1964–1966, before the impulse was squelched by another (fighting) war in Viet Nam. The Clintons' crusade to reform the delivery of health services died aborning.

All this is to suggest that when assessing social work's commitment over the decades to issues of poverty, it would seem wise to recognize that mainstream popular perceptions of poverty and related social problems persisted in being based on a cluster of traditional nineteenth-century values and principles that together constituted a kind of cultural norm: self-reliance; work; thrift; the primacy of the individual and the family; competition; the benign and efficient rule of the marketplace; the constitutional precedence, in a federal republic, of local and state government in matters pertaining to health, education, and welfare; and, implicitly, the assumed superiority of middle-class white citizens. It was not social work alone that operated from racist assumptions. These cultural norms proved remarkably resistant to fundamental modification. Modest forays consistent with (European) social democratic theories and goals had always to contend with this powerful conservative national consensus. For House Speaker Gingrich's "Contract with America" resonated with long- and deeply held American principles and values.

Within such a social and cultural environment, professional social work leaders and educators may have erred, as many of the chapters accurately set forth, but such lapses or misplaced professional emphases need to be understood in this larger historical context.

When I was an apprentice historian, I could always provoke sophomores to laughter with a recital of Calvin Coolidge's axiom that "the business of America is business." Tautological he may have been, but nevertheless close to the objective truth.

A few further passing reflections are in order.

One bears on schooling, on informal understanding and learning of the public at large. Lay citizens know intuitively and from direct experiences the duties that many professional persons perform. Physicians slice and suture and dispense pills. Dentists fill and pull teeth. Lawyers sue you and take you to court; they'll get you if you don't watch out. Teachers teach. These are *known* services, performed well or less well, experienced and observed by everyone as they go through life. Laypersons rarely have such direct experience with social workers, whatever their specified craft. Over a quarter century or so of teaching beginning candidates for the MSW degree, I discovered that few among this self- selected subset of graduate students had a precise idea of what it was that social workers, which they intended to become, really *did*. It may be impertinent to add—because my own published work was rarely clear on these points—that historians of social welfare and of social work have not often or clearly examined in detail the lives of *practicing* social workers, on what really goes on in a public assistance office, for example. The histories we write tend to focus on great leaders, on high policy. We are inclined to deduce from evidence in the *Proceedings of the National Conference on Social Welfare* (and its predecessors), from publications of professional journals, or from learned reports generated by committees of social work associations or by professional educators. These constitute essential records for the historian, of course, but they do not automatically or easily reveal the intricacies of daily practice itself. In my estimate, the "new social history" (history "from the bottom up") has had only a minor impact on the writing and teaching of welfare history. There are some notable exceptions to this generalization, but this is not the occasion to cite such exemplary research.

On this subject, however, I would add a related reflection based on thirty years of studying the literature of what we identify as social welfare history. There are two bodies of literature—one created by scholars whose home discipline is history, another constructed by social work educators who, happily, use history as a focus and function in their academic lives. Over many years I have checked out footnotes and bibliographies evidenced in these two bodies of scholarly work. Historians tend to read and cite the works of fellow historians; social work scholars tend to read and cite the publications of fellow guild members. In the early 1960s, when a coalition of scholars, inclusive of both fields, founded what came to be the Social Welfare History Group (SWHG), the alliance between the two groups was close and strong. Increasingly, however, the two camps have drifted apart—to the detriment of both. It came to pass that the SWHG, once a partnership, fell (in some part owing to the default of guild historians) under the control of social work educators; and its board was led to invent a new office: "Liaison to the Historical Profession." Both parties to the original partnership have suffered from this division, and so has scholarly investigation into the issue of poverty and social work that this volume explores.

Several chapters in this volume have noted, usually with regret, the growing concentration of focus in graduate social work education on psychological disciplines, the decline of academic sociology, the turn to a curriculum heavy on casework with behavioral emphases. Thus are the poor lost sight of, it is claimed. The empirical evidence leads us to these conclusions. An earlier reaching out to academic economics, for example, or to political science and public affairs faded. This is not the fault, if fault it is, of schools of social work alone. The questions generally addressed by academic political scientists came themselves to be specialized and subspecialized and became increasingly irrelevant in method, mode of inquiry, and substance to the needs and capacities of graduate students in social work. Economics as it took flight in econometrics and in modeling the marketplace had less and less to say to social work students (if, indeed, they or their professors were clever enough even to begin to comprehend advanced economic theories). This condition has often been noted and bewailed.

Fewer critics, however, have commented on the loss of humanities disciplines in the background liberal education of students headed for careers in social work. History, to be sure, is tolerated and even cherished in some few schools. Moral philosophy is all but lost, save for a session or two devoted to a review of codes of ethics. One remembers the classic days of the University of Chicago School of Social Service Administration when law, public policy, economics, and history were central ingredients for serious study. One remembers that the authority exercised by Jane Addams and Mary Richmond, to cite but two from the pioneer generation, came in some substantial part from what they had gleaned from reading and studying philosophy, literature, history, the arts, and even religion and theology. They knew how to write in clear and powerful prose, blessedly free of jargon, because they were rooted in basic humanistic and social scientific studies. In this regard it is salutary to peruse the informal essays written by Richmond and collected in *The Long View*, a volume rarely studied, although students know of *Social Diagnosis* chiefly by its title.

But to return to a more explicit discussion of the central concern of this volume—the apparent drift of social work away from its initial focus on poverty and the poor—the chapters devote far more attention to developments within the profession than to the changing nature of poverty itself. The field of welfare history as a subspecialty of social history was opened up and initially defined by Robert Bremner's now-classic volume *From the Depths: the Discovery of Poverty in America*. Historians of the 1930s, Roosevelt, and the New Deal were compelled to describe and analyze the nature of poverty and the lives of the poor during the Great Depression. The "rediscovery" of social poverty in the late 1950s and early 1960s fostered another body of literature, although a comprehensive, definitive synthesis remains to be done. I haven't the wit or space to attempt a survey of the changing nature of poverty over the past century, but it may be helpful to conclude this Afterword with a few observations.

Every measure—gross national product, accumulated capital worth, per capita income in real dollars, standards of living, life expectancy, and the like—has demonstrated an upward trend. The quality of the lives of the poor at the turn of the century in 1900 was quite radically different from the quality of poverty now on the eve of the millennium. At least this would appear to be the case in the United States and other highly modernized societies. Many social, economic, technological, entrepreneurial, and managerial forces contributed to these advances, progress that was unevenly distributed by class, race, and gender it is important to add quickly. As for social policy, we remind ourselves that Old Age Insurance, established at prudent levels in 1935 and expanded incrementally over the next four decades, probably did more to reduce the incidence of poverty in America than any other policy initiative. By 1980 the incidence of poverty among citizens over sixty-five years of age had been reduced from approximately 35 to 12 percent, a rate of poverty that prevailed in society generally. Persons of color, women, and children, as we know, disproportionately represented a poverty population.

The greatest disparities in economic well-being, however, were re-flected in standards generally of the northern hemisphere as opposed to countries south of the equator. Many recent studies, moreover, indicate that in recent decades the distribution of income within the United States has tilted in favor of the rich and to the detriment of low-income segments of the population. The disparity of family incomes between the wealthy and the poor, many have concluded, is greater now than at any time in the twentieth century. Surely these are conditions that should be of concern to social workers as to citizens generally.

One is compelled, moreover, to ponder the radical changes in technol-ogy and globalization of the economy that are transforming the world in our own time. From the earliest days of industrial and finance capitalism, capital enjoyed an advantage of mobility over that of labor. Still, from approximately 1820 to 1920 hard-pressed peasants and low-wage laborers in Europe migrated in enormous numbers to better economic opportuni-ties in the United States, Canada, Australia, and select countries in South America. It constituted a vast folk migration of labor to capital. Beginning in mid–twentieth century, capitalist societies accelerated their transfer of capital to low-wage (poverty) regions of the world—the Pacific Rim, Latin America, the Caribbean, Africa. Transnational corporations shifted invest-ment capital with relative ease and speed in their search to maximize prof-its from the employment of cheap labor in remote regions of the globe, thus stranding many relatively high-wage workers in this country, espe-cially in the textile and electronic products industries but in heavy indus-tries such as steel as well. It goes without saying that highly sophisticated computer technology facilitated the acceleration of these trends.

Consider two agencies, the World Bank and the International Monetary Fund, each more accountable to centers of international capital than to gov-ernments of lending countries; they are understandably more concerned with receiving interest and loan repayment from borrowing societies than with the long-run economic stability and welfare of these states. Terms of these loans typically demand domestic policies from borrowing nations that are likely to lead to greater social inequity. Deepening poverty, sharper maldistribution of income, and social instability flow naturally from such requirements. Jane Addams was a prophet of international peace and jus-tice, but she was spared the task of addressing such complications.

Without further detailed elaboration, it is sufficient for the purposes of this volume to note the impact these developments are having on the extent and nature of poverty, and therefore on the obligations of the pro-fessions, including social work notably, and citizens generally to compre-hend the scope of these transformations and to invent strategies to ameliorate their negative consequences. That task has been rendered more difficult owing to the inability of any nation-state, as they have functioned in the modern era, to establish and implement effective controls. The exploitation of the labor, resources, and natural environments of societies on the Pacific Rim by Western capital, in way of illustration, would seem at the moment to be quite beyond the capacity of either the West or of East Asia to regulate and control. Yet the impact of poverty at either end of the relationship would appear to be a consequence. In the absence of international institutions, save those agencies that are designed to facilitate global exploitation, profound human dislocations are bound to occur.

I raise these points at the end of these reflections, not for polemical purposes but to suggest, as I have earlier, that the definition of social work functions and strategies in regard to poverty and the poor demands an understanding of urgent and fundamental economic and cultural developments and only then, in that larger historical context, can we assay a description and analysis of the response of the professions of human, social services themselves.

And so I close, as the editors of this volume began: "[T]he twentieth century has not been altogether kind to planned social interventions, especially those most clearly related to social welfare. Today we are, as a society, skeptical of our knowledge of human behavior, we are doubtful of our ability to design social change and we are suspicious of professional motivation."

Amen.   Amen.

Index